MATCH PLAY and THE SPIN OF THE BALL

MATCH PLAY
and THE SPIN
OF THE BALL

William T. Tilden, 2nd

New Introduction by
Asher Birnbaum

ARNO PRESS

A New York Times Company

New York / 1975

Reprint Edition 1975 by Arno Press Inc.
Copyright 1925 by William T. Tilden, 2nd
Copyright © 1975 by Arno Press Inc.

Manufactured in the United States of America

Library of Congress Cataloging in Publication Data
Tilden, William Tatem, 1893-1953.
    Match play and the spin of the ball.

    Reprint of the first 12 chapters of the 1925 ed.
published by American Lawn Tennis, New York.
    1. Tennis. I. Title.
[GV995.T6   1975]   796.34'22   75-33763
ISBN 0-405-06679-1

NEW INTRODUCTION

Tennis players dream of raising their performance on court to a new plateau. The average club player will find in Bill Tilden's *Match Play and the Spin of the Ball* several rarely mentioned ways to do that.

Early in his valuable chapter on "The Spin of the Ball," Tilden points out that "every ball has an outside and inside edge every time it comes to you . . . the edge you hit determines the curve and spin of the ball on your return . . . the whole object of putting twist, spin, cut, curve on the ball is to force your opponent into error."

That's quite a change from the major thrust of most tennis books and many tennis lessons: get your racquet back and keep your eyes on the ball.

Tilden does not completely forgo those familiar basics. His version, placing double stress on concentration, cautions: "Keep your eye on the ball and keep your mind on the game."

But today's reader, hungry for a formula that will raise his status from C to B or from B to A, is more likely to be persuaded by Tilden's stern warning: "Never make any stroke without imparting a conscious, deliberate and intentional spin to the ball."

In another chapter, Tilden acclaims "The Value of Intensive Practice." Like the chapter on spin, this discussion of practice should prove inspirational. While neither chapter provides the popular "how to" approach, both are much more likely than most current tennis books to send the reader out to the nearest court with new goals and increased enthusiasm.

Written in 1925 by one of the greatest players of all time, *Match Play* provides an intriguing blend of prophecy and obsolescence. How did Tilden know with such certainty that "the indoor game is rapidly coming to the fore. The time is not far distant when every city of importance will have a fine indoor club."

In the same breath, however, he states that "the indoor game, whether on wood or linoleum, is a game of speed . . . indoor tennis is always handicapped by rather inferior lighting," hardly a prophetic reading of those modern-day indoor clubs that have selected cushioned slow-playing surfaces and near-perfect lighting systems.

For those who consider the Australian formation in doubles a relatively new invention, it will come as a surprise to find it recommended by Tilden as an imaginative approach under the proper circumstances.

Tilden's stress on back-court play and references to now obscure players he cites as examples of particular strokes or tactics are less helpful than when first written. But those references should encourage readers to watch the play of current professionals in a more meaningful way.

His references to Harold A. Throckmorton, Watson Washburn, Zenzo Shimizu and others are more than offset by his discussion of Jo

Gettem, Pete Swattem and Jo Form who still are playing at your club and mine.

If your tennis game is pretty much the same today as it was several years ago and you really want to improve it, *Match Play and Spin of the Ball* will send you back to the court with a new outlook and a new set of goals.

Don't be put off by Tilden's early warning that teaching "professionals are for beginners . . . this book is for the tennis bug, because it is primarily advanced tennis." This book is refreshing because it suggests ways to improve your game that are not commonly stressed today.

If you have uncommon tenacity and unlimited access to court time for experimentation, you may be able to incorporate these strokes into your arsenal without assistance.

Most readers would do well to select a solid teaching professional who can demonstrate the shots that Tilden recommends. After a few lessons, re-read Tilden's chapter on practice so that you'll be inspired to perfect your new weapons. Then it will be time to schedule matches with all those players who have been consistently beating you.

With your new understanding of spin, the relationships of spin, speed, pace and control, you're going to be a much tougher competitor.

ASHER BIRNBAUM
Editor, *Tennis Magazine*

INTRODUCTION

THERE is no sensation in the sporting world so thoroughly enjoyable to me as that when I meet a tennis ball just right in the very middle of my racquet and smack it, just right, where my opponent should be but is not. I enjoy the ring of the baseball off my bat (if I ever manage to hit one), the thrill that comes as the golf ball sails down the course from my driver (it usually sails out into the rough or else ten feet down the course), the thud of the football as it goes (possibly 15 yards) off my toe, the ice under my skates (or my back, more often); but none of these afford me the same mad thrill of crazy excitement as grips me when I smack a tennis ball, "just right."

Just because I am a tennis bug. One of those poor nuts that will sit out, until eight o'clock at night, together with other tennis bugs like Craig Biddle and Wallis Merrihew, to watch a couple of kids, or old men, or dubs, finish a match that means nothing. I am writing this book in the hope that somewhere in the world is another tennis bug who will have as much fun reading it as I have had writing it.

This book is for the tennis bug, because it is primarily advanced tennis. Anyone can go out to a professional and be taught strokes. They may be good or they may be bad (the strokes I mean), according to the professional. My experience tells me that in nine cases out of ten they will be bad. Professionals are for beginners, novices, the Great Dub—to relieve him of his unwelcome burden of that title.

Only an amateur who has been through the mill of championship, competitive tennis, can tell the inside story of tennis, its fine points, its science and its art. It is something of the inside story of match play, from the technical angle, that I am writing.

"BILL"

BY GERALD L. PATTERSON

To Bill Tilden full credit is due for the wonderful progress of the game of lawn tennis in these last five years. His keen, analytical brain has made possible a higher standard in tennis, his writing has given to all lovers of the game a chance to know just why the Spin of the Ball is so closely allied to Match Play.

There are many who conceive that certain tactics will help win a match. In the main this is alright for those who have not reached the top flight, but it is just here that Tilden stands out as the master. He is the only player in the world at the present time who has reached the top flight, for the reason that his *analysis* carries him further than anyone else's *tactics*. This may seem a sweeping statement, but as I have played against him many times I at least know, that, no matter how well I may play on that day, he is always capable of going one better. We do not yet know the peak of his game simply for the fact that no one is now able to force him to the limit.

The reasons for his complete mastery are embodied in his articles, *Match Play and the Spin of the Ball,* for in my opinion they represent those things which are absolutely necessary for successful competitive tennis, namely, suitable temperament and perfect physical condition, while Spin calls for complete Control. Give anyone these three attributes and you have a worthy rival for Bill Tilden.

Bill's preparation for a strenuous tournament season is a strenuous round of Match Play. He has become so physically fit that only a long, forced rest from tennis could impair it. I say "forced," to try and impress that there would be no other reason than sickness which could keep Bill off the place he loves, the court.

When we were playing the Japanese at Providence this year Bill had played an exhibition double with Sandy Wiener and they had been beaten. Not satisfied with telling

Sandy of his errors, he took him out next morning for two solid hours and went over every possible shot with the boy; and every rally was punctuated with remarks which the youngster could not but help assimilate. To do this sort of thing on top of a strenuous season only goes to prove that Bill's physical and mental condition was fresh.

His control is always with him when needed. Words cannot adequately describe how he brings off those superlative backhand drives, while the certainty of his swift forehand drive impresses you most when you try to emulate it.

Unfortunately for Bill, he does most of the writing on lawn tennis. Some players occasionally essay to describe a particular match, but the real personal touch comes from Bill. Modesty demands that every one but himself be mentioned; to read his writings one might be pardoned for saying Who is this fellow Tilden, he doesn't figure in any comparisons. Quite rightly he should not, as he is a peer; but few really know the Tilden as we, his opponents, know him. Only occasionally does someone who really knows Bill get an opportunity to tell the world, and I avail myself of this chance with genuine pleasure.

Bill, both on and off the court, is not only the greatest player but its greatest sportsman, and he is the most worthy master of the game, the best of all.

OUR GREATEST PLAYER

BY RICHARD NORRIS WILLIAMS, 2ND

WHEN discussing the ability of our greatest tennis player, W. T. Tilden, it is only natural that we turn for a few moments to the game itself and find out to what level it has progressed—say when Bill was just beginning his game and playing in the second class of some club handicap event, with a handicap of, say, plus 15-3, and he no doubt did it just like the rest of us mortals. The great players of those days were of the steady kind, what we now speak of as the stonewall variety. Nothing spectacular, playing a rather slow all-round game, very well grounded but more or less of a defensive game, with but little power, especially on the attack. This was the natural development from the pat ball beginning of the game. It had acquired and digested the principles of "safety first". It now needed something new, to carry it on one step higher. This "something new" was personified and came in the person of M. E. McLoughlin; and what he brought with him and gave to the game was the spectacular part, the tremendous power of the attack. The game grows by what each generation of players gives to it; this is then digested, assimilated, into what we call the game of that particular period. Thus it was that when Bill started to get his head just above the great mass of the "also rans" he was confronted with a game that was, no doubt, too greatly devoted to the attack. He, however, had started in the days of "safety first", and being a great student of the game, and the time being ripe, he was able to amalgamate the two at first antagonistic games into his great game of today.

Mind you, when I mention McLoughlin as bringing in the fireworks and Tilden the modern game, I in no way mean to give the impression that they were the only ones that gave anything to the game. Each player makes his little contribution, which is just as valuable to the whole as that which is given by the man that represents the combination of those parts. Ward and Davis gave the powerful service, Wright, Brookes and many others gave different units of the attack, thus making it possible for McLoughlin to combine them and thus bring to a climax that great attacking game.

Just as McLoughlin profited by what went before him, so Tilden profited by what he found. Tilden, however, deserves the greater credit. McLoughlin disregarded part of the past—he was young, full of fire, he would not listen to the wisdom of the ages, he did not stop, look and listen, safety first was nothing to him. Tilden, a naturally great player and a great student, realized the value of soundness as well as of fire, and he was able to combine those two into a game that is far and way superior to that played by McLoughlin.

To a great many readers this will probably sound as very meagre praise. My only answer to them is try it! For a good many years it was thought impossible, and yet Tilden did it.

In a few words, it is just a change of pace, that's all, and yet it's a tremendous stride. He has brought the fireworks down and the safety first up, making it into a far more scientific game. Curiously enough, he leans towards the conservative, and this is said in spite of newspaper articles filled with adjectives which give the impression that every time he touches the ball it becomes invisible from speed. Not that he cannot produce speed; he can and often does; but he waits for the proper time and then produces it when needed.

It is a really wonderful game, an ideal game; a great variety of strokes, easily executed, with very little effort, a great deal of pace and "weight" and the shot admirably placed—just easily waiting for the break or the opening—if the break does not come the opening must, then the execution.

CONTENTS

LIST OF ILLUSTRATIONS

Match Play and the Spin of the Ball

List of Illustrations

MATCH PLAY AND THE SPIN OF THE BALL

CHAPTER I.

THE SPIN OF THE BALL

I

THE BALL AS A SEPARATE ENTITY

MOST tennis players look upon the ball that is used as merely something to hit. It is not an individual, separate factor in their play, like their opponent. They use it as a means to an end. Let me suggest the ball for a moment as an individual. It is a third party in the match. Will this third party be on your side or against you? It is up to you.

The ball will do as it is told. Suggest (with your racquet, not your tongue) that the ball curve this way or that and it obeys. It is the power of your suggestion that determines how well your wishes are carried out.

Every ball has an outside and inside edge

1

every time it comes to you. I admit it is round, yet to the player the side nearest you is its inside edge and that away from you its outside edge; and the edge you hit determines the curve and spin of the ball on your return. Why should we curve or spin the ball?

1. *We do it to gain control of our shot.*
2. *We do it to fool our opponent.*
3. *We do it by accident.*

Let me recommend that you confine your activities to the first two of these, for the third will happen anyway.

Curve and bound will be affected not only intentionally by your shot but quite unintentionally by wind, air friction and poor court surface. Tennis matches are often won by conditions, and the man who is sufficiently master of his game to turn conditions to his account is the one who will usually win. The factor in the game most affected by external conditions of wind, heat and playing surface is the ball. Its weight, bounce, flight, and even size, vary with varying conditions. It is for this reason that the mastery and complete knowledge of spin and curve of the ball is of paramount importance to a tennis player. I prefer to make the ball follow my suggestions, rather than chase it around at those of my opponent.

Let me open this discussion by a sound tennis maxim:

"Never give your opponent a chance to make a shot he likes."

The whole object of putting twist, spin, cut, curve, or whatever term you prefer to describe your control of your stroke, on the ball is to force your opponent into error.

I may sound unsporting when I claim that the primary object of tennis is to break up your opponent's game, but it is my honest belief that no man is defeated until his game is crushed, or at least weakened. Nothing so upsets a man's mental and physical poise as to be continually led into error. I have often seen players collapse in a match after they have netted or driven out a crucial point which they should have won. It is with a view not only to your own stroke but to the effect on your opponent that leads me to say, "never make any stroke without imparting a conscious, deliberate and intentional spin to the ball."

There are two fundamental facts as to spin:

1. *The more spin the less pace, and vice versa.*

2. *Top spin tends to drop; slice or cut spin tends to rise.*

Spin may be imparted either by a long follow-through, which, in my opinion, is the soundest method for all ground strokes, drives or slices; and by a wrist movement, which is preferable in volleying. This latter is essentially a slice or under-cut spin.

Remember, that where a shot is designed to defend the spin should tend to bring the ball toward the center of the court; when a shot is used for attack, the spin can be used to curve the ball either way, according to the direction of your passing shot.

Slice shots tend to curve toward the sideline closest to the point from which the stroke is made, and are thus apt to go out over the side. Top spin tends to curve the ball toward the center of the court.

The slice is a righthand baseball pitcher's "in-curve," while the top spin is analogous to the "out-drop." In hitting a slice or under-cut shot the racquet passes under the ball and inside (closer to the body). The top spin shot is hit with the racquet head outside the ball and passing up and slightly over it.

Every player who desires to attain championship heights must understand the value of spin on the ball. Spin means control. Knowledge of how to use it assures a player of a versatile defense and attack.

The most useful, and, in the main, the most used service carries slice spin. The rotation of the ball causes it to curve and bounce from the server's right to his left, or, in other words, toward his opponent's forehand.

The object of this service spin is to force your opponent to reach for his return, causing his shot to either slide off his racquet or

5

to pop weakly in the air. The spin will tend to make his shot travel down the backhand sideline of the server's court unless he acutely pulls his stroke across court, a difficult and dangerous shot. To offset the natural tend out of the return of this slice service I advocate meeting the service with a flat racquet and imparting top spin by a long follow-through, thus neutralizing the twist of the serve.

The reverse twist, so popular among beginners as something unique in their experience, is not a sound service.

This reverse twist is imparted by hitting the ball from *below* and behind and carrying the racquet up sharply from right to left, with a sharp lifting motion. The ball travels in a high, looping parabola, with a fast shooting drop, which, on hitting the ground hops high to the forehand of the receiver.

The first few meetings with this freakish delivery are apt to be disastrous until the receiver recognizes the hop and the excessive twist away from the curve of the ball—the reason for its name, reverse twist. Once that is gauged, all one needs to do to handle the service is to advance on the ball, meet it at the top of the bound with a firm, fast stroke and a flat racquet face. The twist, still on the ball as it leaves the ground, again reverses and, acting as top spin, holds the receiver's drive in court. I know of no service so ideal to drive hard as the reverse twist.

The American twist, also a reverse as to curve and bound, but far more effective and useful, is one of the greatest assets to a player. It is the service which made Maurice E. McLoughlin famous. It is used by R. N. Williams, Watson Washburn and myself as the foundation of our delivery, although we all mix it up with the slice.

The ball is struck behind the head with the racquet traveling from left to right and up over the ball, imparting a distinct "out-drop" top spin. The ball curves from the server's right to left and bounces from his left to right and high or, in other words, to your opponent's backhand, generally his

7

weakest point. The great twist with which it hops from the ground tends to pull his stroke out over the sideline. For this reason the receiver should always strive to pull an American twist service into court and allow a large margin of safety at the sideline.

I am discussing twists in service in detail because, in service, twist rather than speed is the essential point. It is by twist and placement, rather than by speed, that you can force your opponent on the defensive at the opening of the point. Speed alone is easy to handle. It must beat the other man clean or his return will force *you* on the defensive by your own speed turned back on you. The cannon-ball service, a delivery of which I am supposed to be a leading exponent, is almost without twist, hit with a flat racquet face and quite incapable of control or placement except by accident. Richards, Johnston and Williams, if they can put their racquet on the ball at all, and they usually can, all handle my cannon-ball flat service more easily than either of my spin deliveries. So

8

NORMAN E. BROOKES

Australia

Longwood, 1924

Reaching for a forehand volley. A perfect example of footwork and concentration. Note the right foot extended (Brookes is left handed), the weight under perfect control, the slight curve of the racquet forward to bring the ball back into court, if he reaches it, and the eyes intently fixed on the ball. Some idea of Brookes' genius can be obtained when it is recalled that he was almost 47 years old when this picture, with the vigor and power of youth clearly shown, was snapped. Brookes won the Championship at Wimbledon in 1907 and 1914.

PLATE 1

WILLIAM M. JOHNSTON
United States
Wimbledon, 1923

Hits his forehand drive. A fine example of the power of Johnston's stroke, even though his feet appear to be out of correct position. Evidently the left foot has swung away from its stance as Johnston drove. Note the eyes intently following the flight of the ball, and the tenseness, both physical and mental, indicated in his whole pose. An excellent example of the Western drive grip.

PLATE 2

The Spin of the Ball

I strongly urge, from personal experience, base your service on a twist of some sort.

Let me turn to the use of spin in actual play, once the service has been delivered. Remember that, as a general rule, top spin or a flat, twistless shot is offensive, the basis for attack; while a slice, or under-cut, back-spin shot is defensive. Top spin carries control, speed and pace. Under-cut carries control and direction but no speed.

Against the net man, who is storming the barrier, all passing shots should be hit with top spin. In the first place, top spin will drop more quickly and force him to volley up from below the top of the net. Secondly, the shot carries more speed and as much control as a slice. The reverse of the spin of a top shot when it is volleyed tends to cause it to rise up in the air unless the volley is perfectly hit, while a slice, when volleyed, pulls down off the racquet, often for a kill. There can be no two views about the advantage of top spin over chop or slice against a net attack when striving for a passing shot.

Let us consider the defensive lob for a moment—the attempt to gain time when you are forced off your feet by your opponent's attack. Here the under-cut lob is the better choice. The under-cut tends to hold the ball longer in the air, as the friction of its spin reacts. Also, when struck, it comes down rapidly, often forcing the net man to hit into the net. The slight gain in time itself may give you time to recover your position, even if your opponent makes his kill. Top spin lobs, or the so-called "loop drive," are useful only as a surprise, never as a sound defense.

Admitting the foregoing, the question arises as to spin from the baseline when both players remain in the back court. Here is where the under-cut shot, with its tantalizing hesitation of bound, advances to almost equal footing with the top spin. The top spin will win outright more often than the under-cut, owing to its greater speed and severity, but I am of the opinion that the under-cut shot is more apt to force your opponent into error. There is less labor involved in making the slice shot, while its irregularity of twist is greater than that of the top spin shot, and therefore harder to judge accurately.

The ideal combination is a mixture of the two. Personally, I study my man and lay my attack accordingly. I form the basis of my game on a top spin drive, using the slice shot to mix pace, speed and depth.

Certain players are peculiarly susceptible to error from certain twists. A sliding chop to the forehand of Johnston or Williams is fairly effective, while against Wallace Johnson or Vincent Richards it is a waste of time; yet this shot will almost alone defeat Shimizu or Kumagae.

If I were to lay down a general principle to follow, I would advise slicing to a player who prefers a high bounding ball to drive, and top spin driving to the man who likes to slice or chop his return. It is quite a difficult feat to chop a chop, yet it can be done successfully at times, as Robert Kinsey proved in his crushing defeat of Wallace Johnson in the 1923 Championship.

11

THE SPIN OF THE BALL

2

ATMOSPHERIC CONDITIONS AND COURT SURFACES

ATMOSPHERIC conditions should always be taken into consideration in deciding what twist to use on a shot. It is almost impossible to successfully slice or chop in a high wind, as the wind will catch the floating ball and blow it far out of its intended direction. I advocate using top spin or very little twist of any sort when the wind is high.

The court surface is another factor in determining what spin to impart to the ball. Every court, even those of the same general type of surface, varies, and in fact each court varies from day to day. A soft court, either of grass or dirt, is an invitation to under-cut the shot, as the back spin allows the ball to dig in and die as it bounds. A hard, fast court should be recognized as the paradise for the hard-hitting driver. This fact accounts for the great speed of the Californians on their forehand top spin drives, since they play all year around on asphalt.

The grass court surface is best suited to the mixed spin game, since on the average good grass court a man may drive or chop with equal success, while on any other surface that I know one form of spin is partially nullified by the nature of the bound.

On grass, dirt or hard court the drive or top spin shot will bound reasonably high and with a distinct forward pitch to the flight. This means an offensive attacking shot on any surface. It is the slice or under-cut spin which varies according to surface. On grass the chop or slice shot drags or shoots according to the amount of back spin or side spin imparted. No surface provides such an excellent result to this shot as grass. Heavily under-cut back spin drop shots will fall almost dead, while the stinging slice of Wallace Johnson will shoot viciously low and hard into the defense of his opponent. On dirt or clay the chop or slice carries some shoot, but very little drag or hesitation. It is apt to bound high and soft, asking to be driven for a kill by the waiting player. I consider a chop or slice stroke player at a distinct disadvantage on the dirt court, while on such surface as concrete, asphalt, wood or linoleum the chop and slice are useless except as a defensive method of returning speed.

Only a few grades of dirt courts, notably the En-Tout-Cas, have a surface that will provide a real chance for the full use of the under-cut spin. It is to be hoped that these types will be developed in the United States as they have been in Europe.

I think that I have drawn the picture clearly of why I advocate the use of top spin ahead of under-cut, yet I feel that both should be in the repertoire of every player. There is a place when a certain type stroke is the only one to meet the situation, and if that situation presents itself you should not be without the stroke to meet it.

14

The Spin of the Ball

I cannot too strongly urge that the spin used on every shot should be a deliberate, conscious thing. Do not hit a ball blindly, merely for the sake of hitting it somewhere. Have a clear-cut idea of what will be the effect of that shot. Never await your opponent's return with mind a blank. Ask yourself what you would do in his place and prepare to meet that reply. Anticipation in tennis is nothing more or less than outguessing, or at least, equi-guessing, your opponent.

A slice to either corner will tend normally to come back more or less straight down the line, because it requires special efforts to pull it 'cross court. A drive will be capable of being returned either way, but you know your opponent's favorite shot, so watch for it. Spin that holds the ball low on your return tends to make your opponent's shot high when he returns it. Conversely, your floater will probably return fast and low. Seek always to place your opponent at a disadvantage by forcing him to guess your shot's spin and so make it more difficult to handle it.

Let us consider how the great stars have handled spin in the construction of their games.

The most astute master of spin, and the man who utilized it to the greatest advantage, was Norman Brookes. This fact has been borne in on me in every match I ever played Brookes, and I have played him many times.

No matter how I disguised my intention of receiving his service he always twisted the ball so it was bounding into my body when I made my return. Always he forced me to make my own opening to stroke. He saw I was too large to like a shot close to my body and so he based his attack on this point. Forehand or backhand, he made me play my return of service stepping away from the ball. This was done by a supreme command of spin.

George Church, the old Princeton star, held that every shot should carry spin. His ground strokes, weak in themselves, lacking pace and speed, carried so much twist that he could carry his attack to the net back of them, when a man less skilled in the knowledge of the effect of spin would have been caught helpless, halfway to the net.

Watch the ball sizzle from the strings of Johnston's racquet and watch its action off the court. Every shot of Johnston's carries a hidden devil in the form of spin or twist. That little wrist movement on his volley, so slight as to be hardly noticeable, carries just the little added twist that forces the volley to victory past the waiting opponent. Johnston, ever aware of his lack of weight, has carefully utilized every available asset in building up his game. He has developed timing nearly to perfection, and he then deliberately places twist or spin on his shot.

Watch the sharp, incisive slice to his seemingly mediocre service, and realize that that is the reason his opponent is often aced.

Note the ripping forehand, with its magnificent top spin for control; or the vicious sliding chop stroke that glides away from the racing player in pursuit; and recognize the fact that all that is a deliberate and conscious application of spin.

No one can look at Billy Johnston's slight frame but who will marvel at his pace and speed; but he wins many matches by cleverly mixed spin.

Two of the cleverest exponents of the value of spin on the ball are the Kinsey brothers, Howard and Bob. In fact, their whole games rest on spin. My opinion is that they have over-emphasized spin, and by so doing have lost pace and speed; yet each wins many matches by cleverly mixed spin.

Let me make my position perfectly clear on spin. I believe every shot should carry a definitely defined spin, or lack of it; but I do not believe in excessive or exaggerated spin on any shot. Make all your strokes with enough spin to gain control, or to gain the desired reaction from your opponent, and then put the rest of your effort into speed and pace.

I am a great believer in the flat drive from the baseline as a foundation. When I say "flat," I mean a top spin drive with just as little top spin as it is possible to put on and still top the ball. That gentle rotation will control a shot from the baseline and still not detract from its pace. The shots which, in my opinion, should be hit with distinct spin are short passing shots when your opponent is up (use top spin on these), or a heavily under-cut drop shot, or high defensive lob.

My mottoes in tennis are "the maximum result for the minimum effort" and "always work to break up your opponent's game." The first of these can be obtained with the flattest possible shot, but the second is only possible by mixing with these flat drives a careful and judicious series of shots with various spins.

I am unalterably opposed to freak shots. I consider that any soundly constructed game will break up and easily defeat any of the freak types. I cannot imagine the peculiar forehand styles of Shimizu and Kumagae standing up to the pounding of a Johnston, if it were not for other factors than their mere strokes. Excessive reverse twists, underhand cut services, elaborate but ineffectual contortions in any stroke are affectations.

Watch the play of Johnston, Richards, Williams, Alonso (barring his service, which is his weakest link), Gobert, Norton, Cochet, Patterson, J. O. Anderson (barring the backhand of the two Australian stars, also their greatest weakness), and where can you find a grotesque or awkward movement? These men hit their shots naturally, easily, gracefully, placing the spin on the ball in moderation and with consciousness of effect. Theirs is the fluency of mastery, the beauty of style that only command of their game and science can give.

Why should a novice strive for more than the master, yet why should he be satisfied with less? Control of spin, just like control of stroke technique, is a matter of study and practice. Many players have wonderful shots, yet have not mastered the knowledge of which to use under any given situation.

No one can lay down a set rule to follow. Only experience and one's own brains can direct successfully the destinies of a match player, yet a knowledge of the science of spin and its effects is a big step forward.

The old card maxim, often a fallacy, "When in doubt, lead trumps," may be paraphrased for the tennis player to read, "When in doubt, drive."

Remember, that your defense is no better than your attack, so base your matches on your offensive. Do not sacrifice speed to freak shots, yet, above all, do not hit blindly for the sake of speed.

It's a wise child who knows his own father, but it's a wise tennis player who knows his own stroke, knows it not only in its swing, but in its spin, in its intention and, above all, in its probable return.

In closing the discussion of spin I feel that some slight description of the effect of spin on speed and pace should be given.

Speed and pace are not the same. They

are totally different. Speed is the rate at which a ball travels through the air. Pace is the momentum (rate of speed, plus the player's weight) with which it comes off the ground. Thus a fast shot that has not the player's weight in it does not carry pace when it comes off the ground. Conversely, some shots travel comparatively slowly through the air, but by virtue of the player's weight behind them come off the ground with pace.

I have said that the more spin the less speed, but that does not necessarily mean the less pace. Certain spins impart pace, provided the weight is kept in the shot. It is of spin in relation to pace that I would draw your attention. The flat drive undoubtedly carries the most pace for the least effort, but it is also apt to lose control. The top spin drive will carry more pace than the undercut, because the twist, at the moment of impact with the ground, shoots forward, while the undercut drags and slows up. The value of spin, well used, is to change pace and lead the other player into error.

The Spin of the Ball

There are times when a slow dragging shot is absolutely necessary to produce the effect desired, where top spin would come off the ground too high and with too great a forward bound. The time to use this drag shot is against a tiring player who has reached the point where it is an effort to reach for a stroke. On the other hand, there are times when only top spin of a flat drive will carry the ball beyond the opponent's reach. If you have driven your opponent far to one side and then hit to the other side for the point, use top spin, for it will jump off the ground with pace, thus allowing him less time than if you under-cut it and drag the bound.

In volleying, the sharply blocked, slightly under-cut volley shoots off the ground with greater pace than the plain stop-volley or heavily chopped shot. When hitting deep for a clean earned point meet the ball sharply and impart a side spin that carries the ball away from the other player. This is particularly true for cross court volleys. Short stop-volleys may be safely under-cut and heavily dragged so the ball will not rise high on the bound and will have little forward movement.

Every man uses spin to his own individual taste and to suit his style of game. Many great players use it almost unconsciously, at least subconsciously. One cannot set down hard and fast rules to follow, yet the principles I have outlined will be sound as a general rule.

In closing my discussion of spin I am attempting to show how it is used by the great stars of today. Modern tennis ranges from the almost spinless game of J. O. Anderson to the over-spun game of the Kinsey brothers, and each extreme has some particular virtue.

Never discard any tennis game as useless until you have studied it. You will usually find something well worthy of your attention and imitation somewhere in the stroke production.

VINCENT RICHARDS
United States
Forest Hills, 1924

Volleying a low backhand. Note that he has not assumed correct foot position but his weight balance, with the weight forward on the left foot and in the stroke, is perfect, so that, as a born "timer," he violates footwork yet obtains correct balance. Note his eyes watching the ball almost on the racquet, and his left hand extended to preserve his equilibrium. His position in court is faulty. He is almost on the service line when he should have been several yards closer to the net.

Plate 3

JAMES OUTRAM ANDERSON
Australia
Forest Hills, 1923

The famous forehand drive of the great star of the antipodes is here shown at its start. Note the beautiful footwork, free swing of the arm, the flat racquet face, and the eyes intently watching the ball as it comes to him. Many critics rank Anderson's forehand as the greatest in the world.

PLATE 4

THE SPIN OF THE BALL

3

HOW THE GREAT PLAYERS HANDLE SPIN

CIRCUMSTANCES alter cases and individuals alter rules. When you come to study the games of the leading stars you will find that many of them violate every rule I have outlined as the laws of spin. I may be wrong. All I can do is to stand on my own ideas and then outline briefly the way in which other men use spin. Let me make one statement, even at the danger of offending some of my friends. I do not believe there are many men who consciously think about spin in their game, for the great majority of tennis players are not students of the game. It is the love of study of tennis that has led me to the point where I never hit a shot without a conscious application of twist or the deliberate attempt to use none. I believe that only by so doing can the greatest results be obtained. I think there are many great players whose games would be materially improved if they gave a little more thought to the matter of spin and its effect.

William M. Johnston is a man who imparts a great deal of spin to his strokes. His service carries a sharp slice that causes the ball to shoot to the right when it hits the ground. His forehand drive is struck with more top spin than the average, which, coupled with his weight behind the shot, causes the pace off the ground. When Johnston chops off his forehand, which is seldom, he does so with excessive under-cut spin. All Johnston's volleys are sliced, which partially accounts for the sudden shoot of the bound. Even his overhead is hit with spin rather than speed. The most outstanding use of spin in Johnston's game is off his backhand. This shot, considered by many a weakness in his game, actually is very dangerous. True, he tends to slice the ball rather than drive it, but he uses his weight so well in his shot, and carries through so far on his swing, that the shot has many of the virtues of a drive and few of the defects of a chop. The racquet passing *inside* the ball, imparts a sliding curve and bound to his left that is a hard shot to handle. I cannot say that I believe Johnston to be a deep student of spin; I think he uses it more by unerring instinct than by deliberate thought. Some few men have subconscious control that is as good as conscious thought, and Johnston is one of them.

R. N. Williams, 2nd, is far less a producer of spin on his strokes than Johnston. Williams uses spin, both slice and American twist, in service, but in volleying (except on his stop-volley) and in driving (except occasionally down the line) Williams makes most of his strokes as flat as possible. I would consider that Williams consciously eliminates spin wherever possible from his game, except in service or in the more or less "trick strokes." This is one reason for Williams' bad days. The flat drive must be hit absolutely correctly or it is wild. If

Williams is not hitting his flat shot perfectly, if his eye or his footwork is off, he is apt to be far below his best form. Spin would allow him a greater margin of safety, but he would lose some of his startling brilliance. I believe spin when used by Williams is a deliberate, conscious application.

Vincent Richards is a player who uses spin on every shot. He has no flat shots in his game, except an occasional overhead. This is one reason why there is a lack of speed and pace to Richards' ground game. He has even discarded top spin from his game. Every shot, except an occasional wild lift drive off his forehand—a shot I have repeatedly urged him to discard for a more normal drive—is hit with under spin. He slices his normal forehand and every backhand. He slices his volley, overhead and service. It is only because he mixes the amount of slice with great cleverness, couples it with an uncanny sense of anticipation and unerring judgment in advancing to the net, that Richards is the great player that he is.

It seems to me that any player with Richards' tennis intelligence should recognize the fact that he can never gain the top and hold it unless he learns a top spin and flat drive. It is the difference in ground strokes between Johnston and himself that always throws the balance of victory to Johnston. One spin alone, no matter how cleverly mixed, will not avail against the very best of men.

One of the most striking examples of the foregoing statement is Wallace F. Johnson, the great chop stroke star. There is no finer student of tennis tactics, nor complete master of the under-cut spin, nor more crafty, subtle and determined fighter in tennis than Wallace Johnson. Yet, the defect of his limited stroke equipment, the complete lack of the fast drive, has always held him just a shade below the championship. Some men, like Johnson and Richards, sacrifice speed to spin. Others, like Williams, sacrifice safety to speed. A player of the latter type is James O. Anderson of Australia. There is a complete disregard of spin, an utter flatness to his game, that seems to me to need adjustment. Anderson's marvelous flat forehand is a far better shot than Richards' chop, yet why should not Anderson couple with his flat shot one that carries top spin for safety to use when pressed? Anderson is like Williams in the fact that when he does use spin it is almost excessive, usually on some trick shot. Even his service, volley and overhead are hit flat—marvelous when right, but prone to error if he is slightly off form. I believe that there is a happy medium between the narrow margin of safety of Anderson and Williams and the too wide margin of safety of Richards and Johnson. I think that Billy Johnston has found it. Manuel Alonso and Brian Norton are very near it. It is the middle road of spin plus speed. It is the road I seek to travel myself.

There are many other interesting figures in the discussion of spin. Manuel Alonso is a player who combines, in the main, the best of spin. There are places, I think, where he overstresses spin. He seeks to put too much twist on his service and his volley, yet I think he perfectly adjusts his spin on his ground strokes. Alonso is a student of the game, working to improve his weakness. I believe that he is gradually removing excessive spin from his weaknesses and will eventually become one of the great masters of the game.

Brian I. C. Norton is a player who imparts spin with skill and cleverness to his game. His use of the right amount of spin to a shot is far better than that of many men who defeat him. The defect in Norton's game is not in his mastery of racket technique. Norton mixes top spin and slice and flat drives with a nice sense of proportion. If he emphasizes the American twist service at times, it is usually a spirit of experimentation that has him in its grasp. Norton is a victim of his own moods— moods that often beat a game that for sound stroking and use of spin is one of the best in the world.

One of the most interesting exponents of spin, almost a victim of twist, is Zenzo Shimizu. The Japanese star, due partially to his small stature, and partially to his faulty racquet grip, is required to rely on spin to win for him. He cannot chop or slice with his grip, nor could Ichiya Kumagae, his countryman, so that these Oriental stars developed the excessive top spin shot which has become recognized in the past few years as the lob-drive. It is nothing more than an exaggerated offspring of the old Lawford stroke. Shimizu (and to a great extent Kumagae), based his game on the amount of top spin imparted, thus varying his pace by changing the amount of spin he put on the ball and by the trajectory plane of his shot. Only by the consummate knowledge of that spin and the indefatigable court covering ability of these Japanese players were they able to gain the position they attained in the tennis world.

John B. Hawkes of Australia is a player who is handicapping himself by too much

JEAN BOROTRA
France
Wimbledon, 1924

The Bounding Basque bounds after a backhand volley. Note the eyes on the ball and the beautiful footwork, with the body poised on the toes like a dancer.

PLATE 5

THE EASTERN FOREHAND DRIVE GRIP

William T. Tilden, 2nd, illustrates the orthodox grip for the flat forehand and top spin drive. In the Eastern grip the opposite face of the racquet is used for fore- and backhand shots, the grip changing one-quarter circle on handle.

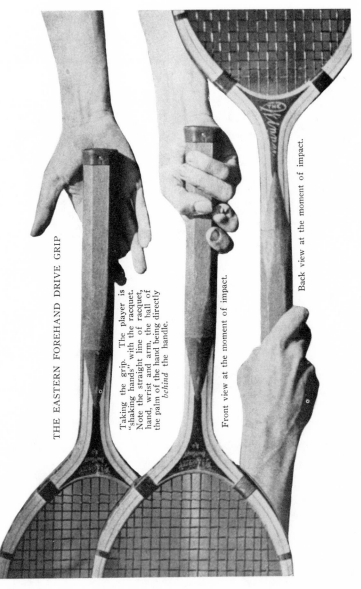

THE EASTERN FOREHAND DRIVE GRIP

Taking the grip. The player is "shaking hands" with the racquet. Note the straight line of racquet, hand, wrist and arm, the ball of the palm of the hand being directly *behind* the handle.

Front view at the moment of impact.

Back view at the moment of impact.

PLATE 7

THE EASTERN FORE-HAND VOLLEY, SER-VICE, AND CHOP STROKE GRIP AND SLIGHTLY EXAGGER-ATED ENGLISH FORE-HAND GROUND-STROKE GRIP.

Front View—Note the dis-tinct angle at wrist, the rac-quet head well above the wrist.

Front View — Note the marked angle at the wrist in contrast to the straight line of both Eastern and Western backhand drive grip.

Back view of the forehand volley.

THE EASTERN BACKHAND VOLLEY AND CHOP-STROKE GRIP

PLATE 8

spin. He over-tops his drive, he slices his backhand too much and almost breaks his back by imparting exaggerated American twist to his service. I should think that, owing to the fact that Hawkes is a left-hander, this exaggerated twist in service would place a very severe strain on his heart. I cannot see why he uses so much spin, for he has developed under the eye of Norman Brookes, who, while one of the greatest exponents of spin in the game, never used an exaggerated stroke or wasted movement. Brookes utilized spin for the definite purpose of forcing his opponent to err. He did not consider spin the end, but only the means to an end, which was to force his opponent to net or out. Every stroke of Brookes' either broke into his opponent, if the unfortunate victim disliked a ball close to him, or away from him, if the other disliked to reach. Brookes was always the master mind of tennis, and nowhere was it more clearly demonstrated than in his use of spin to break up his opponents' games. Hawkes seems to consider spin the end, not the means to that end, a fallacy he shares with the Kinsey brothers.

Gerald L. Patterson utilizes spin for control of his great speed. He, like Hawkes, over-emphasizes it, but not from the same reason. Patterson is gradually working around to the flat drive on his forehand and is in a very interesting evolution on his backhand that passed from the exaggerated top spin of his "loop," to the heavily sliced shot of his last American visit.

Let me sum up my conclusions on spin:

I. The more spin, the less speed, and vice versa.

II. Every shot should be hit with a definite spin, or lack of it.

III. Top spin tends to drop, slice or cut spin, to rise.

The Spin of the Ball

IV. We should use spin:

    1. *To gain control.*

    2. *To force our opponent to err.*

    3. *To change pace.*

V. Study the games of the leading players and learn why they use spin and how.

CHAPTER II

GRIPS

GRIPS, hand clasps, seem to have a peculiar fascination for mankind. You meet a perfect stranger for the first time and immediately seize him by the hand and pump his arm up and down vigorously as a sign of interest. Groups of individuals form societies and immediately pick out some peculiar grip as a symbol of their undying fidelity. Even the movies indulge in long "grips" at the end of the picture, but these are not necessarily confined to the hands. However, grips have their recognized place in civilization, and among the most important grips (other than suit cases and La Grippe) are the various grips on a tennis racquet handle. Many players do not realize the importance of correct grip in relation to stroke production.

There are three general styles of grips; all others are modifications of these:

Grips

1. *The Eastern Grip, used by such stars as Vincent Richards, J. O. Anderson, B. I. C. Norton, Norman Brookes, myself and others.*

2. *The Western Grip, represented by William M. Johnston, Howard Kinsey, George Lott, Harvey Snodgrass and others.*

3. *The English, or "Continental," Grip, used by Rene Lacoste, Jean Borotra, A. R. F. Kingscote, Henri Cochet and, in a slightly modified degree, by R. N. Williams, 2nd.*

Certain great players combine the grips using two or more styles. Manuel Alonso uses a Western forehand and Continental backhand, while Gerald Patterson hits his forehand with an Eastern grip and varies his backhand between the Western for his "loop-drive" and English for his slice. There is merit to every grip, if you can once find which shot is best suited to which grip. Certain styles of play need certain methods. Let me attempt to outline the grips, a thing which will be far better illustrated by the accompanying pictures than by my writings.

The Eastern Grip. It is changed for forehand and backhand drive and on the volley. The forehand and backhand shots are made on different faces of the racquet. The forehand drive grip is best acquired by holding the racquet as if it were standing on the edge of the frame, the short strings perpendicular to the ground, the handle pointing toward you. Then "shake hands" with it. The ball of the thumb and the wrist are behind the handle, the fingers and thumb curve around it and settle comfortably in place. The wrist is locked stiff at the moment of making a stroke and the grip is tight at the impact of the ball on the strings. The line of the arm, wrist and racquet is straight. There is no angle in the correct Eastern grip.

The backhand drive grip. In making the change from the forehand drive grip to the backhand drive grip, imagine the racquet remaining in the same position, then turn the hand backward (counter-clock-wise) on the handle for a quarter circle (12-9 on the clock). This will bring the hand directly on top of the handle, the fingers and thumb

38

curve around it, the wrist above the handle locked stiff, and the arm, hand, and racquet again form a straight line. I do not advocate the thumb up the handle; personally I do not use it, but if it gives a sense of security to any player then by all means let him adopt it.

The volley grip and service grip are just mid-way between the forehand and backhand drive grip. It is also the grip for the slice or chop. In fact the Eastern slice or volley grip is practically identical with the English drive grip. In this grip, the wrist is always below the racquet head, thus making a distinct angle at the wrist, between the hand and racquet. In all Eastern grips the forehand shots are played on the opposite face of the racquet from the backhand.

The Western Grip. There is very little, if any, change between the forehand and backhand grips in the Western style, and none for volleying. The shots are all hit on the same face of the racquet. To acquire the Western grip, hold the racquet with the face parallel to the ground (the exact opposite of learning the Eastern grip), and then drop the hand on top of the handle. When the racquet is brought back to the same position as used in learning the Eastern grip, it is found that for the forehand the hand is further *below* or *around* the handle than in the Eastern, and by using the same racquet face on the backhand as forehand the hand then is not quite so much on top of the handle as in making the Eastern backhand. The Western grip insures automatic top-spin on a forehand but tends to produce a slice on the backhand. It is a fine grip for deep fast volleying, particularly off the backhand, but tends to cut down variety of finesse, since delicate stop-volleying is difficult with it.

The English grip, already described as the Eastern volley or service grip, half-way between the Eastern drive grip, provides for the broken line, the angle at the wrist, and, to me, appears unsound. Forehand and backhand shots made with the English grip are hit on opposite sides of the racquet face.

Grips

My belief is that all great players vary their grips often, according to the shot they are playing and the spin they intend to put on the ball. I know that while the foundation of my game is based on the Eastern grip, I often use a Western forehand grip to obtain a certain spin on a forehand drive, while for certain sliding shots I will use an English grip. Johnston is not uncompromisingly Western in his grips, nor is Alonso always Continental. Every player should have a certain definite foundation for his style and then develop along the lines that best suit his physical and mental equipment. I am a great believer in individualism in tennis, so long as it has the sound foundation of form behind it. Work out your own racquet grips along your personal views, just so long as you have a safe, sane theory to fall back upon in time of stress.

Look at the hundreds of freak shots that one sees in tennis today. All these are made with an unorthodox grip. Yet, behind them is usually a sound foundation. The strange forehand of the Japanese is the result of a light ball they formerly used in Japan that has modified their Western grip. Howard Kinsey is changing his grip all the time as he experiments with new developments of his loop shot. He may find something radically different in grips if he keeps up his experimentation—or he may ruin his own game. Time will tell.

Unorthodox grips produce unorthodox shots and unorthodox shots will never win tennis matches. They are very useful for one given point. They may even win throughout a set, but only sound, sane, sensible tennis will succeed in these days of scientific development of our players. Beware of the unorthodox grip for anything except an ornament to your structural foundation of form. Be sound, be sensible, be sane—and be Champion. Every year that goes by I am working closer to the middle road of Controlled Speed and Orthodox Form, and I find my reward in increased steadiness and power.

CHAPTER III

FOOTWORK AND TIMING.

SPIN and its many varied problems are closely related to one of the fundamentals of tennis which few people thoroughly understand, viz., Footwork and Timing.

Footwork is the means to perfect weight control and balance.

Timing is the transference of the player's weight into his stroke, thus giving "pace" to the ball.

Good footwork is the secret of success in boxing, baseball, tennis, football, dancing and many other sports, for by this medium the punch of the boxer, the carrying power of the batter, the pace of the tennis player, the distance of the punter, or the balance of the dancer is determined. There is a fraction of a second when ball and body are in such a juxtaposition that if the ball is struck then the speed and pace are increased over any other time of playing. That is the moment when the weight of the body crosses the center of balance in a forward movement, simultaneously with the ball in its backward flight, and the stroke and ball meet. Only by this forward movement of the body weight at the exact moment of striking the ball is it possible to acquire the maximum power. That is perfect timing.

Some few people are born with the sense of perfect timing. Babe Ruth owes his "home run" reputation to it. Glenna Collett obtains her distance by it, Billy Johnston's terrific forehand is due to it. W. C. Fields extracts comedy from juggling through it. Mary Garden thrills thousands by the drama of her use of it. Perfect timing in sport, art, or science is the same thing, and through it people produce the sublime in their particular field of endeavor.

Unfortunately, most people are not born with the gift of perfect timing. In art it is almost impossible to acquire but in sport, through the medium of footwork, it may be learned so well that in time it becomes almost second nature. I know whereof I speak, because I was not born with a sense of perfect timing; yet by careful study of the laws of footwork I have succeeded in learning a degree of proficiency in timing. Therefore it is to the other unfortunates who, like myself, were not blessed with the gift from the gods, that I am offering my views on footwork and timing.

Most players do not know why they miss shots. In many cases they are not aware of the most common cause of error, not watching the ball. Certainly, few players realize that they are almost always on the wrong foot for a shot; or, if fortunate enough to be correctly placed as to feet, they have allowed their weight to take root on the wrong foot. I know many first flight men who invariably are on the wrong foot, or with their weight placed in the wrong position for certain strokes. Gerald Patterson seldom is on balance for a backhand stroke. Wallace Johnson fails to throw his weight into his volley. Watson Washburn seldom has his weight behind his overhead, and so it goes on down the line.

There are two general rules of body position so elemental in tennis that I almost feel I should omit them from this book, but to make this chapter complete I must restate them.

(1) *Await a stroke facing the net, with body parallel to it.*

(2) *Play every stroke with body at right angles (sideways) to the net. This is true for service, drive, chop, volley, smash, half-volley and lob.*

It is with these two points firmly fixed in mind that I turn to the actual question of foot position.

In awaiting a return the feet should be well spread, the weight evenly distributed well forward on the toes, so as to insure a speedy turn to either side. The moment the direction of the oncoming return is determined, the shift of position to sideways to the net must be made. For all forehand shots the left foot should be advanced toward the right-hand sideline of the player, thus bringing him sideways automatically. For all backhand strokes, the reverse order is used, the shift causing the right foot to advance toward the left sideline.

This formula is perfectly simple for a stroke where one step forward is required to reach the shot. It is the shots that one must run after which require the careful study. Let me state a most important and, wherever humanly possible, invariable, rule:

A player should always have his weight travelling forward at the moment of making a stroke.

This is true even if he is forced to run backwards to reach a ball. He should throw his weight forward with his swing as he strikes. There are two absolute rules of footwork that will never fail.

1. *To reach for a ball advance the foot that is away from the shot. For example, for*

a forehand drive, advance the left foot to the ball.

2. To back away from a ball retreat the foot that is nearest to the shot. For example, for a forehand drive, retreat the right foot from the ball.

If one is required to chase a shot the run should be so gauged that the player arrives at the ball with his left foot closest to it in the case of a forehand and vice versa for the backhand. Most players think that foot position has nothing to do with stroke production, but anyone who desires proof of the value of footwork should study the methods of William Johnston, Manuel Alonso, Vincent Richards and Brian Norton. The ease and fluidity of stroke of these men is in sharp contrast to the more labored style of such faulty footwork exponents as Lindley Murray, Watson Washburn, and Frank Hunter.

Only by correct footwork can perfect timing be acquired. The born expert in timing, like Johnston or Richards, may violate the

THE EASTERN BACKHAND GRIP

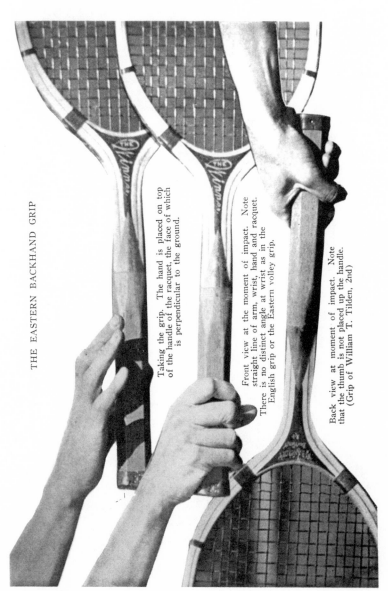

Taking the grip. The hand is placed on top of the handle of the racquet, the face of which is perpendicular to the ground.

Front view at the moment of impact. Note straight line of arm, wrist, hand and racquet. There is no distinct angle at wrist as in the English grip or the Eastern volley grip.

Back view at moment of impact. Note that the thumb is not placed up the handle.
(Grip of William T. Tilden, 2nd)

PLATE 9

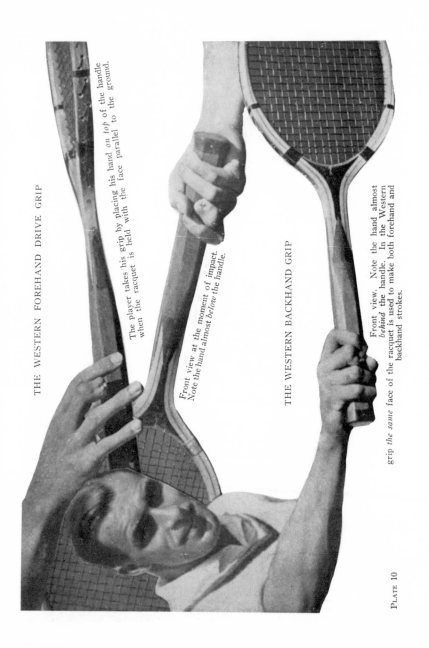

THE WESTERN FOREHAND DRIVE GRIP

The player takes his grip by placing his hand *on top* of the handle when the racquet is held with the face parallel to the ground.

Front view at the moment of impact. Note the hand almost *below* the handle.

THE WESTERN BACKHAND GRIP

Front view. Note the hand almost *behind* the handle. In the Western grip *the same face* of the racquet is used to make both forehand and backhand strokes.

PLATE 10

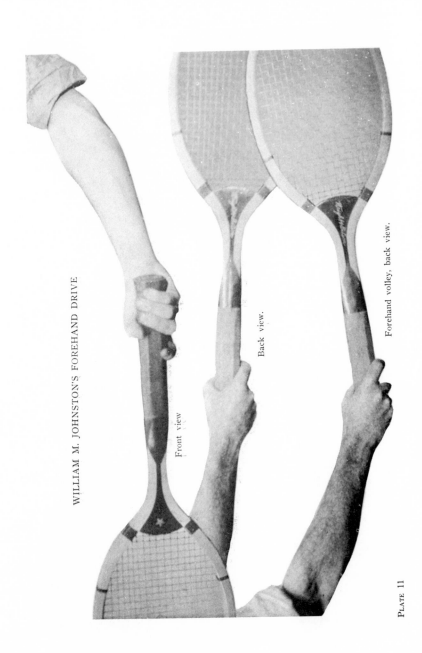

WILLIAM M. JOHNSTON'S FOREHAND DRIVE

Front view.

Back view.

Forehand volley, back view.

PLATE 11

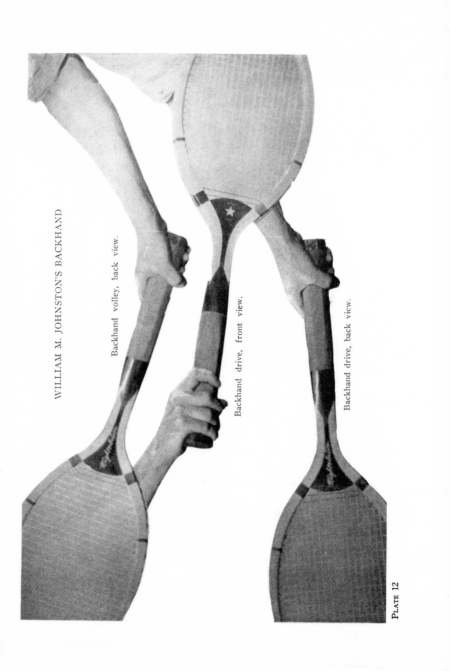

WILLIAM M. JOHNSTON'S BACKHAND

Backhand volley, back view.

Backhand drive, front view.

Backhand drive, back view.

PLATE 12

rules of footwork because, without changing the position of their feet, they control their balance and weight placement by instinct; but with the exceptions of these few born "timers" the only certain method of timing is by good footwork.

Let us consider the stroke made with the feet incorrectly placed, so that the player is facing the net. The swing must be made around the body, not in the line parallel to it and along the flight of the ball. Obviously, the combination of the face of the stroke and the pace of the ball is so difficult as to be almost impossible, since the tangent (or the flight of the ball) touches the circumference of the circle (of the swing of the stroke) at only one point. There is but one chance in so many that I can say that a well timed shot in such a case is more an accident than an evidence of skill.

On the other hand, in the case when the player has advanced his foot into the shot, thus turning him sideways to the net, the swing is practically a straight line parallel to the body and directly along the flight of the ball. Consequently there are many chances to meet it squarely. The perfectly-timed shot is the one that is hit just as the weight shifts forward from the rear to the front foot; but even if the shot is not perfectly timed, at least it has many chances to be hit clearly, whereas in the former case it has only one. Watch Johnston, Anderson, or even Hunter at times when they hit their mighty forehand wallops. They square off sideways and almost jump from back to front foot with their shot. It is this perfect weight shift that allows Johnston, one of the smallest men in the tennis world, to hit a ball harder than almost any other player.

I do not recommend the jump-shift of weight to the average player. Only a thorough master of the game and an experienced "timer" can afford to leave his feet to impart "pace" to a shot, for unless perfectly timed he loses rather than gains by his jump. The average player should learn correct foot position, plant his feet firmly and then shift his weight with his stroke without leaving the ground.

I know many players who understand correct footwork, yet who cannot cure themselves of a most peculiar form of bad timing. These men approach a ball, make their stroke and as they complete it bring their feet into correct position, thereby absolutely losing the body weight behind the stroke, which was made before they have turned sideways. Yet when you protest to them and tell them they hit off the wrong foot they argue with you and point with pride to the position of their feet at the completion of the stroke. Correct footwork demands that the feet are in position and the body sideways to the net before the stroke is commenced. The most flagrant violator of this rule among the first class players is Williams, but his smooth stroke-production often saves him. Sandy Wiener is one of the players who reaches correct foot position at the end of a stroke instead of the beginning, one cause for his errors off the ground. It is easy to understand why the delayed placement of the feet in correct position is fatal, because by this delay the body weight is not travelling on the same line nor at the same speed as the swing of the stroke and therefore cannot be utilized in the shot.

I have a peculiar method of insuring correct footwork when I am forced to run for a shot. It is a trick and, as such, requires practice to master. To reach a shot far away on my forehand I run directly for the shot until about six feet from the ball, when I make a little "skip step" that turns my body sideways to the net and (in the case of a forehand) brings my left foot toward the ball well in advance of my right, so that when I land after my skip I am in position to make my stroke at once. If I have failed to judge my distance correctly, I repeat the "skip step", thus keeping my body in correct position for the stroke. In other words, once I am within a possible striking distance of the ball, and until after it is struck, I am careful to be sideways to the net at all times.

My stroke once made, I allow my follow-through to pull me along with it so that at the end of my swing I am once more facing the awaiting return. The real secret of court covering, footwork and timing is judgment of distance, and the ability, once that distance is covered, to reach the ball with your feet in correct position.

The value of small steps, "skips" and what many of the uninitiated call "showing off" by dancing into position, cannot be too strongly commended to the real student of tennis. Watch Brian Norton pirouetting around on his toes before he makes a stroke. Many people dismiss it with a contemptuous "Babe is showing off." They are wrong. He is manoevering for correct foot position and balance. The large, and at times ponderous, bulk of Washburn is splendidly handled by small steps, as he dances into position. Richards uses dozens of little skips and steps in working his body out of the way of his arm as he volleys. Jean Borotra looks like a ballet-master or Premier Danseur, but for all his acrobatic contortions, he is a wonderful exponent of fine footwork. Footwork in tennis is identical with footwork in boxing. The weight should always be thrown forward with the punch, but to dodge, turn, or start, the weight should be equally divided on the toes of the feet.

Certain great players have idiosyncrasies of footwork that are individual to them, yet based along the foundation of scientific theory. I have already mentioned the seemingly incorrect foot placement of Johnston and Richards, due to their inborn sense of balance that allows them to control their weight without the actual foot movement. Both men have marked faults or virtues of footwork that stamp their game with an irremedial trademark. It is the perfect footwork of Manuel Alonso, who seems strung on wires as he glides around the court, that lifts him above the defect of a faulty racquet grip on his backhand. The slight weakness of Rene Lacoste on his forehand is due quite as much to his tendency to face the net as he strokes as it is to incorrect grip or faulty swing. The corresponding strength of his backhand drive is due to the beautiful footwork that brings his body into every stroke he makes from his left side. It seems strange that Lacoste should have two styles of footwork, one good and one poor, from the baseline.

Jean Borotra, like Lacoste, has far better footwork on his backhand drive and in volleying than he uses for his forehand groundstroke. Borotra is catlike at the net, and also from his left side from deep court, yet he is often caught almost flat-footed on a return to his forehand.

Gerald Patterson and R. N. Williams, 2nd, are the two great players who seem to violate every rule of footwork and, at times, get away with it. I am convinced it is poor footwork that is the underlying cause of Williams' lapses in timing and resultant "bad" days. I have watched and studied Gerald Patterson, with the ultimate conclusion that faulty footwork is at the bottom of the almost inexcusable errors with which Patterson breaks down at critical periods of matches.

Only Patterson's indomitable will and courage has carried him above the inherent weakness of structure of his game. Patterson is always facing the net off his groundstrokes. The ball is on him, often before his stroke has gained headway. He is driving from his heels repeatedly. Only his tremendous physical strength allows him to obtain the speed he does. In marked contrast to his execrable footwork from deep court is his perfect style and timing on his service and overhead smashing. The outstanding fault of one stroke is remedied and becomes the crowning glory of another. There is no finer example of perfect rhythm and coordination of body and feet than Patterson's marvelous smash.

In marked contrast to Patterson's footwork in driving is the flowing grace of his teammate, Pat O'Hara Wood. I know of very few players who cover a court with less effort or in more correct style than this Australian. He seems always to be on the

RENE LACOSTE
France

Forest Hills, 1924

The start of a high backhand volley made in perfect form and perfect
position. An excellent example of the studious nature of Lacoste's tennis.
By the time the ball is struck his right foot will be in position and the
racquet will be advanced to meet the ball.

PLATE 13

HENRI COCHET
France
Wimbledon, 1923

A magnificent example of weight control and footwork for a low volley or half volley, the left arm being used as a balance pole to steady the body.

PLATE 14

ball, with body sideways to the net, hitting with a free swing that is a model of beauty. Only Norton, Alonso, Richards and, at times, Johnston equal the ease of O'Hara Wood's stroke production.

Every player should find some definite theory of footwork that suits them and work on it. Personally I have evolved my "skip step" and believe in it, but while I explain it for others to try I do not urge them to adopt it as an essential of good footwork. Any method that insures weight control, and the body out of the way of the player's swing, will suffice to produce results. The more natural that action is to the given player the easier it will be for him to master it.

Most players crowd the ball on all their strokes. I cannot too strongly stress the advice, "do not crowd your strokes." Crowding the ball hampers your swing, reduces your pace on the shot, cuts down the accuracy, reduces the range of direction, cramps the muscles and fatigues you. *Keep away from the ball.* Allow yourself ample room to swing freely and to provide the long follow-through. It is better to overswing than to underswing, and crowding the ball tends toward an underswing. Regulate your footwork so you avoid crowding your stroke.

Many players follow too closely the well known fact that a straight line is the shortest distance between two points. That is always true, but sometimes the shortest straight line to the ball is actually the longest chance of making your shot. Let me explain by an example:

A player is forced to his forehand sideline, about the service line, to make a recovery. He hits deep to mid-court and his opponent, obviously, will drive deep for his backhand corner. The shortest line to the flight of the ball is directly across the court, along the service line; yet that is the wrong defense to use. In the first place, your position is bad if you reach the ball at all, which is unlikely; in the second place, you will be forced back as you stroke; and finally, if you make your stroke, you are again caught in mid-court.

There are the other two choices, the net attack or the baseline defense. The net attack under this play, is so hazardous as to amount to certain defeat, since if you cannot be sure to reach the ball at the service line, your chance is still less at the net. Therefore, I claim, retreat to the baseline because,

(1) It allows you more time for the longer flight of the ball;

(2) It allows the chance of error by your opponent;

(3) It provides you additional time, due to the chance to play the ball off the bounce and not off the volley as the mid-court or net position requires.

Therefore a run back! Do not run back to the spot where you think the ball will bounce, since that will require you to half volley it, a most difficult shot. Most players run for the place they expect the ball to strike. I say you should aim for about ten feet behind the baseline and, once you have made up your mind, run fast. Do not make the mistake of loafing back. It is far easier to arrive too soon and wait than it is to arrive too late and watch the ball bounce past you against the back stop. Run directly back and then, still running, turn forward and sweep into your stroke, carrying your whole body-swing into your stroke. In other words, here are the three possible ways of covering the court and timing this stroke.

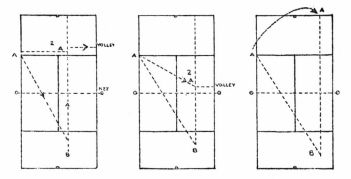

THREE WAYS OF DEFENSE
A. The volley from the service line.
B. The volley from close in.
C. The drive from behind the baseline.

There are very few shots off a bounce that a player cannot run around to hit with his weight coming forward. Once in a while he will be caught so he cannot actually come in with his shot, but in that case he can throw his weight forward with his stroke at the exact moment of meeting the ball. This is particularly true in the case of the volley and half-volley, which often must be played so quickly that the player has not time to move his feet. In the case of diagram C, if the line of "A's" defense continued on the backward line without the turn toward the court just previous to hitting the ball, then it would be poor court covering, footwork and timing. It is the turn and advance to the shot that constitutes the correct method of play.

Richards is the outstanding figure in the United States as an exponent of perfect weight control and balance on a tennis court, coupled with his judgment of distance. It is a gift born in him, for Richards is not a student of tennis. I have watched him very carefully for years and I have seldom seen him make a shot that, at the moment of playing, his weight is not travelling along its flight. He is uncanny in his ability to get behind a ball and come in with his stroke.

One of the few flaws in Manual Alonso's

game is his inability to avoid being caught going backward by a deep shot. It is due more to over-anxiety and over-eagerness to attack, than an inherent inability to time the ball, for Alonso is a wonderful example of perfect footwork and weight balance.

Let me sum up my rules for Footwork:

1. *Await a return facing the net.*

2. *Play every shot sideways to the net.*

3. *To reach a ball advance the foot that is away from the shot.*

4. *To get away from ball retreat the foot that is closest to the shot.*

5. *The weight must always travel forward with the stroke, no matter in what position you are playing.*

CHAPTER IV

ATTACK AND DEFENSE

A CHAIN is as strong as its weakest link— and no stronger.

In these days of modern tennis a player is as strong as his weakest stroke. The old days of the one-stroke player, the lop-sided game, are gone forever. Today a player to reach the top must have everything. Therefore, in this particular chapter, I am going to throw to one side any question of the relative ability of the players, admit they are equal in stroke equipment and turn to the vital question of the use of strokes.

Many a great match is won because the victor used the right stroke at the right time; and, conversely, many a championship has been lost by the player who picked the wrong stroke in the pinch. The most beautiful stroke, from a technical standpoint, is useless if it is hit to the wrong place at the wrong time; while often a sloppy-looking shot, to the right place in the court at the critical period, has swung defeat to victory.

Wallace Johnson once snatched victory from Stanley Pearson at match point, with Pearson leading one set-all, 5-1, and 40-15, by hitting a feeble backhand shot down the line while lying flat on his face. It was the right shot at the right time, and Pearson blew up from surprise and Johnson won. Vincent Richards won the Mexican Championship in 1923 from Manuel Alonso by a sensational volley at match point against him. George King lost to Howard Kinsey in the 1924 Championship of the United States by the wrong shot, a missed drop volley, when if he had hit deep he would have won, as he was leading 2 sets to 1, 5-3 and 30-all. R. N. Williams, 2nd, threw away his match to Brian I. C. Norton in 1923 in the United States Championship by netting an easy volley, with Norton far out of court when Williams was leading 2 sets-all, 4-1, and 40-15.

One could go on citing hundreds of cases where one shot in the pinch won or lost a match, but the point which I am about to take up is not merely the one shot at the psychological moment but the question of the correct shots to play throughout a match. I am afraid that at times in this chapter I may be repeating some of the matter I used in the portion of this work devoted particularly to the Spin of the Ball, but the reason is the close relation between spin and the whole question of attack and defense.

There is no use arguing about the relative values of Attack and Defense. I have heard some players claim that attack, and attack alone, is the objective at which to aim. Others say a sound defense is all one needs. It is just as ridiculous as to argue about that as to argue whether a perfect baseliner can defeat the perfect volleyer. There are no such "animals."

If there were, the perfect baseliner would beat the perfect volleyer in six love games because, by the definition of either perfect style, the baseliner would pass the volleyer every point. You cannot volley the service, and therefore the perfect baseliner would have one drive, which would win before the perfect volleyer could volley.

There is no attack without defense, and no defense will succeed without attack. If one were to classify the players who have specialized on one style at the expense of the other you would have some such line-up as this:

GROUP ONE

The Attackers—Maurice E. McLoughlin, R. Lindley Murray, Richard N. Williams, 2nd, Harold A. Throckmorton, Gerald L. Patterson, Jean Borotra, Carl Fischer.

GROUP TWO

The Defenders—Howard O. Kinsey, Robert G. Kinsey, Charles S. Garland, Wallace F. Johnson, Zenzo Shimizu.

GROUP THREE

The Combination—William M. Johnston, Vincent Richards, Rene Lacoste, Henri

Cochet, Watson Washburn, Francis T. Hunter, James O. Anderson, Pat O'Hara Wood, Manuel Alonso and myself.

In offering this classification I do not mean to say that the first group has no defense nor the second group no attack; only that one style is predominent in the first two groups, while in group three the two styles are about equally used.

Sometimes a man will change from one group to another in a season or two. Howard Kinsey in 1924 is verging on joining Group Three, and so is Williams; while Billy Johnston could be considered a candidate for group one. This classification is purely my personal opinion and for the purpose of future reference.

Let me, therefore, classify the strokes in tennis as Attacking, or Offensive ones, and Defensive ones. The Attacking strokes are the drive (off the ground), the smash, the volley, and, at times, the service. The Defensive strokes are the chop, the lob and the half volley.

Under certain circumstances defensive shots may be used for attacking purposes but attacking shots, except the drive, can never be used for defense. From the above classification of strokes it can be seen that the style of the players' stroke production practically decides in which group he should be placed. The Kinseys, in doubles, have developed a defense lobbing system that amounts to attack, yet even in their hands the lob still remains primarily a defensive stroke. Wallace Johnson is another player who turns the lob to attacking use once in a while, but these men are the exceptions that prove the rule.

Most players have the firm conviction that the only way to meet an attack is by a counter-offensive so severe that the attack breaks down; or that a defense can be shattered only by wearing the defending player down by greater steadiness. This is an absolutely wrong conception of tactics. Let me once more quote the most useful of all tennis mottoes:

Attack and Defense

"Never allow a player to play the game he prefers if you can possibly force him to play any other."

"Never give a player a shot he likes to play."

Obviously, by playing a man at his own game you are giving him shots he likes to play and which, in nine cases out of ten, he can play better than you. Meet defense with attack, and the attack with combined attack and defense. Note that I include attack in both cases, for only by attack can the winning punch be put across.

Let me take the method of playing against that bane of all tennis players, the *goat-getter par excellence,* the Pat-Ball Artist—in other words, Old Jo Gettem, who never misses anything. The familiar species of *genus homo,* who thrives and abounds at all tennis clubs, is the fellow who scrambles all over the court and pushes, shoves, pokes and pats back shots until you want to murder him. This is the man who annually supplies about three-fourths of the upsets that enliven the tennis world. He is a particularly deadly enemy to young players who have more strokes than brains and experience.

Believe me, it requires more than a wallop to beat Old Jo Gettem. Certain very essential facts must be borne in mind by the player who is spending the afternoon playing Jo in a match, if the player is to have any chance of victory.

First, you cannot go out and just hit old Jo off the court, because you cannot win enough hitting everything to make up for your errors. The only way to hit successfully against Jo Gettem is to wait your opportunity—and when it comes seize it.

Second, you cannot try to outsteady Jo too long, because you will miss before he does unless you hit severely enough to force him to error.

Third, you cannot kill every shot Jo hits to you because his strokes are so soft and cleverly placed that few of them give you a real chance to hit them hard.

Therefore in playing old Jo Gettem you must be patient, steady until an opening comes, and then severe. In other words, you meet defense with defense until you find an opening that insures success in attack. What is an opening against this defense? Old Jo will give you several of them, some of which may pass unnoticed unless you are on the lookout for them. There are the openings of driving Jo 'way out of court, to one side, and hitting hard to the other; and the shot which pulls him to the net so you can pass him, for old Jo Gettem is seldom a good volleyer. But one often misses other openings against Jo because on the face of things they do not appear to be openings. Every once in a few shots old Jo loses his depth on his return and hits to your midcourt. This is an opening and should be seized at once. Drive deep to one corner or the other of the court and advance to the net behind your shot. Once there, volley to kill at once.

There is an opening with service, not one to use every time, because old Jo will learn it quickly, but one to use at discretion. Serve wide and come to the net unexpectedly. It will often break up old Jo, because it hurries him. In that little point lies the secret of playing old Jo Gettem and all his tribe. Hurry him! Whenever, wherever and however possible, hurry the Pat-Ball Artist and you will find he is easy to beat, for he can not make his shots if he is hurried.

Old Jo Gettem has a first cousin, young Pete Swattem. Young Pete is the local hopeful at tennis clubs, "who will someday certainly be a Davis Cup star." He may be the son or some close relation of old Jo Form, but at least he is decidedly young Pete Swattem. You cannot miss him. He is usually tall, wiry, and very peppy. Often he has held the captaincy of the High School team in the past or won the singles championship of Smackemville. Actually he is far from dangerous at the given moment, but strange to say, the valuation of him as a future Davis Cup star may not be far from correct if young Pete Swattem learns tennis sense.

GERALD L. PATTERSON
Australia

Wimbledon, 1922

The Melbourne man at the top of his tremendous service, the most perfect
style of delivery in the world.

PLATE 15

R. N. WILLIAMS, 2nd
United States
Wimbledon, 1924

Runs fast to make a low backhand drive. His feet are not yet in position but the fine rhythm of his motion and his intent concentration on the ball indicate the success of the coming shot.

PLATE 16

Young Pete Swattem is a far better tennis player potentially than old Jo Gettem, yet old Jo will smear young Pete regularly. Once in a while young Pete hits a streak when all his swats are going in, and he beats a really good player.

The reason young Pete only does this on his good day is because he does not know enough tennis to use his strokes correctly on the days when his swat is not going in. There are many young Pete Swattems among the near-great of the tennis world. I passed through a five-year period as a leading member of the young "Pete Swattems" and recognize it, with regret, in others. Young Pete wallops every shot. Service, drive, volley and smash sail off his racquet, singing. Usually the backstop persuades the ball to stop, if not it is the net that succeeds in doing so.

Yet for all this young Pete is dangerous, because if his shots go in they are winners very often. Therefore, in playing young Pete you should rely largely on defense, allowing him to pile up the errors off the backstop or in the net. Only if he hits a streak and his shots are going in court consistently should you attack, and then only long enough to upset his game. Young Pete Swattem thrives not upon returning the ball. He seems to join Lady Macbeth in her famous soliloquy, "Out, damned Spot! Out I say!"

Unfortunately for the defending title holders and aspiring champions, every man you play is not Old Jo Gettem nor yet Young Pete Swattem, nor even Old Jo Form. Some of them are TENNIS PLAYERS (apologies to Mr. George Ade for the use of his copyrighted capitals). These are men who either force you to learn something about combined attack and defense, or else place you quietly in the discards of the Also Rans, saying, "Mah Jongg" or "Chow" or some other strange-sounding word as they do so. Some of them even use the cryptic message, "I double four spades," but these are not real tennis players.

PAT O'HARA WOOD
Australia

Seabright, 1924

The Victorian hits a forehand drive. A beautiful example of perfect footwork. Note the left foot extended toward the ball, the flat face of the
racquet coming into the shot, the eyes fastened intently on the ball in its
flight. One of the most perfect examples of the start of a forehand I have
ever seen.

PLATE 17

HOWARD O. KINSEY
United States
Forest Hills, 1924

The Californian completes his characteristic and unorthodox loop drive.
Note the unnatural strain on the arm, the peculiar grip and the faulty
footwork of this stroke, in marked contrast to the excellent form shown
by him in most of his shots.

PLATE 18

Let me take my method of playing a Tennis Player, in contrast to meeting Old Jo Gettem or young Pete Swattem. My first rule is "Take the offensive at the earliest possible moment." If you are serving you should attack with an aggressive service. If you are receiving, you should strive to make your first return sufficiently aggressive to force your opponent into defense. There is only one thing worse than handing over the attack to your opponent and that is an absolute error. Therefore I qualify my statement concerning returning service to make it read, "sufficiently aggressive to force your opponent into defense, provided first you are certain to put the ball into play." Since 80% of all points in tennis are lost by errors and not won by earned points—and by this figure I mean average tournament tennis—I find it impossible to overstress the slogan "Put the ball in play." Therefore, if your opponent's shot is sufficiently difficult to give you the choice of a likely error in attempting an aggressive stroke, or of putting a defensive shot into play, I advocate putting the defensive shot in play.

My only variations of this rule are when your opponent has perfect net position, or when you are thrown hopelessly out of position to make a difficult recovery, with little chance of comeback into court and play the next return. In these two cases I say take a chance on an offensive shot to win outright. The only defensive shot worth anything under these two cases is a very high lob that will provide you time to come back to court, and this is so difficult to make that I advocate the attempt at a winner.

Few players realize the value of the shots you miss in the pinch. They have just as distinct and definite a value as the ones you make. Many a missed stroke at one time, wins another later by its effect on your opponent. Let me point out what I mean. Your opponent draws you far out of court with a short shot angled to your forehand. He expects a defensive lob or at best a floating return down the centre of the court.

You come and drive it hard along the line. It hits the tape of the net and fails to go over, or it goes over but out the baseline by a few inches. An error and a lost point— but its near-success shook your opponent, who next time will come in, not quite so confidently and wondering if you will make that shot. The result is often that if you do put up a lob or a high cross-court return the net man is caught off balance, because he was watching for the shot you almost made the previous time.

I have set a great valuation on missed shots. Just as I strive to break my opponent's confidence by making, or almost making, the shots that he does not believe I can reach, so also I would rather destroy his confidence by forcing him into error than by winning outright myself. Nothing destroys a man's confidence, breaks up his game and ruins his fighting spirit like errors. The more shots he misses, the more he worries and, ultimately, the worse he plays. That is why so many players are said to be "off

their game" against me. I set out to put
them "off their game." A good tennis player
plays matches just as well as his opponent
allows him. A tennis player who knows his
game may be "off" one day through illness
or accident, but never over a series of matches, unless his opponent puts him "off."

I consider that double faults, missed "sit-
ters" (easy kills) and errors on the return
of easy services, are absolutely inexcusable
and actually tennis crimes. The difference
between the great stars—Johnston, Richards
and J. O. Anderson—and the second flight
men, a shade below them, men like N. W.
Niles, Watson Washburn, Robert Kinsey,
George King, etc., is that the former never
miss easy shots at the crucial moment in a
match, while the latter often throw victory
away by a costly error in the pinch. All
great tennis players miss ridiculously easy
shots, shots that a "dub" would blush to boot,
but the difference between the Champions
and others is that the Champions seldom if
ever miss in the pinch, while that is the

moment the other players break down. In other words, the Champion's defense stiffens under strain while that of the others cracks.

I have played and watched Johnston over a period of five years, under the strain of international competition in Europe, Australia, and the United States, and only once have I seen him blow an easy shot in the psychological moment of a match. That one was his netted kill against J. O. Anderson in the fourth set of the 1923 Davis Cup Challenge Tie, which if made would have given Johnston a commanding lead to win, but when lost ultimately cost him the match in 5 sets. I have seen Johnston beaten, but never except that time have I seen him miss a point that he should have made when the error was vital enough to cost him a match. It is a marvelous performance for any man to go through five years with such match-playing qualities, and it speaks eloquently of the courage of Johnston.

In marked contrast to Johnston's record is the heart-breaking series of costly errors in

big matches of R. N. Williams, 2nd, a series
that have kept him from attaining the pin-
nacle of the tennis world in the last five years.
It is not due to lack of courage that Williams
misses in the pinch, but rather in too-great
daring, and in too-great a willingness to
take unnecessary chances in the pinch when
safety and certainty would win just as well
and fare more surely. At Wimbledon, in
1920, double faults in the pinch sent Williams down against Mavrogordato. In 1921,
in the Championship of the United States,
daring shots to the side line that just missed
their goal beat Williams against J. O. Anderson. In 1923, Williams led Norton 4-1 and
40-15 in the fifth set of their match in the
United States Championship and netted an
easy drop shot when any sort of a shot over
the net would have beaten Norton, who was
hopelessly out of court. There is a big lesson to be learned from the records of Johnston and Williams. It is that the safe and
certain shot in the pinch, when the opening
is there, is the one to play. Do not take un-

MANUEL ALONSO

Spain and United States
Germantown, 1923

This picture splendidly illustrates the wonderful poise of Alonso's footwork.
Note the left arm extended in balance, the right foot used as a rudder, the
long sweep of the right arm in its follow-through. The faulty "Continental" or "English" backhand grip is plainly discernible, counteracted by
Alonso's mobility.

PLATE 19

ZENZO SHIMIZU

Japan

Forest Hills, 1921

A perfect illustration of the peculiar grip and delivery of this popular
Japanese star hitting his forehand drive.

PLATE 20

FRANCIS T. HUNTER
United States
Beckenham, 1923

Reaching for a forehand volley. A fine example of controlled weight and keen visual concentration on the ball. A magnificent shot. Only his racquet grip is **wrong** for a volley. Apparently he stroked his return.

PLATE 21

MAURICE EVANS McLOUGHLIN
United States
Forest Hills, 1916

The California Comet, popular hero, National Champion 1912-13, making his forehand drive. Note the Western racquet grip, the eyes on the ball, and the potential power of the stroke.

PLATE 22

necessary chances when an error may spell defeat, but make sure of your victory when it is in your hands.

Many players who have a sound defense and a good attack never arrive at their best because their judgment is faulty on what shot to use at any given time. I have seen players go out and use the wrong tactics throughout an entire match and afterward not know why they lost. One of the most common failings in tactics is the one of over-hitting against a player with better average pace than you.

We will suppose you are playing a base-liner, as you are, too, and that he has a slighter harder drive than you. You drive, in return, a shade faster than his shot. He drives back with added speed but does not come in to the net. The next shot is the crucial one and, incidentally, is the one on which the mistake in tactics is always made. It is always played even harder than the preceding ones. In nine cases out of ten, it will be missed by the player with the less pace. The correct way to play the shot is to defend it, either drive it high and slow or, better yet, chop or slice it deep. The reason for this is that your opponent may be fooled by the change of pace, and even if he is not, he is required to make his pace all over again, a thing few hard drivers like. The average hard hitter prefers speed, at least average standard pace, to drive against, and mixed speed, spin and pace confuse him.

The most glaring example of a player who is consistently caught and led into the error of over-hitting is young Sandy Wiener. He does not yet know when to defend a ball and when to hit it. In marked contrast to Sandy is young Emmett Pare, who seems born with the sense of when to attack speed and when to defend it.

There is another time when many players are led into the mistake of attack instead of defense. That is when they are being run across the court from corner to corner. The average player will chase back and forth, driving a medium pace mid-court drive back almost into the hands of his waiting opponent, who relentlessly chases him on and on. The correct defense is either a high, deep slice or drive that slows up the pace; or, better yet, a high deep lob. This will allow the chasing player time to return to position and stop running. The only other alternative is to hit out for a winner off a drive, into one corner or the other, relying on speed and surprise to beat your waiting opponent. The mid-court drive I mentioned first is not defense, because it is too fast; and it is not attack because it is not fast enough. It is neither fish, flesh nor fowl. The chop or slice is better defensive tactics than the drive against a baseliner who is running you but not forcing the net, because it is slower in flight and, incidentally, requires less effort to make; but just as soon as you find a chance to wrest the offensive from your opponent, discard the chop or slice and drive your way to attacking position. One cannot defend, except by a lob, against a net player; nor can a net player ever defend at the net.

Once a player takes the net both men are at once forced into the offensive and must hit for the point at the earliest possible moment.

Johnston and I play each other from the baseline because we each fear the other's ground stroke too much to come to the net indiscriminately, but in every point we are sparring for an opening that will allow us to take the offensive and carry it to the net position. I can say that our matches are an example of sound defensive tennis on both sides, with each of us holding an attacking mental viewpoint. That, to my mind, is the ideal type of tennis, ready to attack yet sound in defense.

The first essential of either attack or defense is to learn to keep the ball in play; therefore, it is far better to hit deep and take a chance of putting the shot out than it is to play too short and net the return. There is always the chance your opponent will play a shot that is going out, so give him that chance. I know of no one thing in tennis wearing more to an opponent or that gives you more confidence than to consistently put the ball in play off service. I believe the secret of the success of Vincent Richards against me is the return of my service. He handles both my fast one and my kick with ease and I am always forced to fight long and hard to win my service games, a fact that tends to make me underhit, play too cautiously and lose confidence.

It is Johnston's return of service against Patterson that spells certain defeat to the great Australian whenever they meet. Much of the success of Rene Lacoste of France lies in his ability to put the ball in play off service. Many of the defeats of R. N. Williams, 2nd, R. L. Murray, Watson Washburn, Jean Borotra, Gerald Patterson, and other great players can be traced directly to their inability to return service in that particular match.

The return of service is a comparatively simple matter. There are only a few times when anything difficult must be accomplished with the return of service. Naturally, if your opponent is following his service to the net, then something of actual import is demanded. You must either put the ball slow and low at his feet, or fast enough to pass him out of reach as he advances. These are real accomplishments, yet they are seldom demanded because there are few players who force the net behind their service.

There is the even more exceptional player who has one stroke from the baseline, so strong that you dare not let him use it. He forces the receiver to put the return of service away from the strength, again an actual accomplishment. There are only a few such players. I would say the two great examples are J. O. Anderson and W. M. Johnston, each with a forehand drive. The average player serves and stays back on the baseline. He has no punishing point-winning stroke. The receiver knows this, yet how often will you see a player net or out his service return by trying to do too much with it? I claim that the receiver should allow himself a margin of at least two feet above the net and place his shot deep but with a margin

ROBERT LINDLEY MURRAY
United States
Forest Hills, 1916

The Champion of 1918 is seen camped at the net ready to volley a ball that is coming to him in such a way that he must hit it up.

PLATE 23

GEORGE MYERS CHURCH
United States
Forest Hills, 1916

Donor of the Church Cup and one of the greatest masters of spin, making
a backhand stroke.

PLATE 24

of several feet inside the baseline to insure safety. It is deep enough to put your opponent on the defensive, yet safe enough to allow for a margin of errors. It is not essential how you hit it there. You should preferably drive it, but it will be just as effective to keep the ball in play if it is hit with a chop, slice, poke or in any other way. The point at stake is to put the ball into your opponent's court. Once the service is put in play then comes the time to jump to attack or to fall back on actual defense—but at least put the ball in play and give yourself a chance.

Important as it is to return service in singles, it is vastly more important to learn to return it accurately in doubles, because in doubles every return of service must be an attempt to place the opposing team on the defensive, so as to allow you to take the attack and carry it to the net. In doubles, the return must be low and often short and soft. It is almost impossible to win outright by a service return in doubles. The reason the

Australian and European teams are superior to the American teams, on the average, lies in the return of service, which is so perfected that the partner of the receiver may stand in to jump in to attack when the server defensively volleys the return of service. There are very few American stars whose service return allows a partner to stand in with confidence. We are the superior in service and in volleying of any country in the world, but our return of service is far below the standard, and until that is brought up to the level of the net attack, our doubles team will meet defeat. Only by sound service return can a team wrest the offensive from the service, and doubles is a game of attack, attack and still more attack, in which defense is used to wait the moment to attack. Paradoxically, this very necessity of attack by both teams builds strongly for defense.

Therefore, I say that in singles the main error of many players is the lack of knowledge of when to defend and when to attack.

In doubles we of the United States suffer

ROBERT G. KINSEY
United States
Forest Hills, 1924

The elder brother making a low forehand volley with the care that distinguishes his game.

PLATE 25

A. R. F. KINGSCOTE
England

Beckenham, 1923

The Internationalist at the moment of striking the ball for his forehand
drive. Note the cramped position of the arm, due to the fact that the
feet are not in position. It is seldom Kingscote is caught with bad footwork. He evidently has already struck the ball, which is seen leaving the
racquet, and his eyes are already centered on his opponent.

PLATE 26

through our lack of an offensive return of service behind which we can advance to the net to attack.

In both games the importance of keeping the ball in play cannot be too strongly emphasized.

Chapter V

SINGLES AND DOUBLES

FEW tennnis players know that singles and doubles are different games. They think all you need to do is to play the same strokes in the same way in each with equal success. They believe that successful tactics in one will prove successful tactics in the other. Nothing could be further from the truth. Singles is essentially a game of speed, punch, brawn; while doubles is a game of position, finesse, subtlety. Obviously, the same tactics and strokes cannot succeed in both games. They must be varied and modified to meet the demands of the moment.

Singles tactics are comparatively simple. There are several general lines of attack to follow.

I. Run your opponent until you break him physically. This requires a baseline driving game that will have as its foundation corner to corner drives.

II. The Crushing Attack. This demands speed, speed and then more speed. Hit tremendously hard off the ground and follow to the net to volley or smash for a kill. A most effective method if all your shots are working just right and your opponent allows you a chance to make your shots; only remember that should he succeed in balking your attack you must look out that you do not become a victim to plan Number I.

III. Break up your opponent's game. This is the most subtle of all tactics and requires the greatest skill, because it calls for a combination of controlled speed and a mastery of spin and pace that few players possess. This is the modern all-court game at its highest development. It is the closest approach to doubles tactics found in the singles game.

One can pick outstanding figures of each of the three methods.

I should pick Zenzo Shimizu, Wallace F.

Johnson and Robert Kinsey as splendid examples of Plan I.

Maurice McLoughlin, Lindley Murray,
Gerald Patterson and "Dick" Williams, 2nd,
as the leading exponents of Plan II. "Billy"
Johnston, Vincent Richards, Manuel Alonso,
Rene Lacoste and myself among those who
follow Plan III.

Where speed wins in singles, placement
must win in doubles because there are fewer
and smaller openings in the doubles court
with its two court-coverers than in the singles
court with its one. In singles, usually, you
have an opening for which to hit, on the first
or second shot. But in doubles you can seldom force an opening under three or four
shots. In singles the opening automatically
presents itself, while in doubles you must
manoeuver your opponents out of position, by
clever placement, before an opening presents
itself. In singles, except on the rare occasions
when a man follows his service to the net, the
return of service should be high and deep,
and, in the main, ground strokes should follow

92

the same general idea except when actually hitting for a kill. In doubles, with both server and partner at the net, the return of service and consequent ground strokes must be short, low and usually soft, in an attempt to prevent the attacking team from obtaining a chance to volley down for a kill. In singles the drive should be flat and fast, in doubles it should be heavily topped to make it drop sharply, and should not carry too much speed except when it is hit for a kill. In singles one can often hit for a kill off service, but in doubles the first return should always be played to put the ball in play. In other words, doubles is one shot advanced over singles in every point and usually several shots. Singles is essentially a baseline battle with net trimmings. Doubles is a net battle with a baseline and an aerial defense. There is no need to take the net in singles until the opportunity presents itself to advance with little risk. In doubles you should risk everything to gain the net at the first possible chance.

Let me run over the list of strokes and the

difference in their use in singles and doubles:
Service:

Singles: It is used for attack, an attempt to score aces but, if missed, merely a method of putting the ball in play so the point can be fought out from the baseline. It is seldom followed to the net.

Doubles: It is of the most vital importance to win your service and to do so you must come to the net behind it on every serve. Therefore one should attempt fewer aces but should strive for a higher degree of average effectiveness than in singles. Doubles service requires less speed but more spin than in singles.

The Drive:

Singles: The drive should be flat, fast, deep and high as a general rule, the object being to keep your opponent far back in the court on the defensive and cause him to run as far as possible.

Doubles: The drive should be low, short, heavily topped, slow, and angled so as to force the server to reach for his volley as he comes in, and to make it difficult to volley at any time. Only at a clean opening should the flat fast drive be hit regularly. Ground strokes should be used to make openings.

The Chop:

Singles: A most effective shot for defense and for change of pace, invaluable as an auxiliary shot to the drive.

Doubles: Almost useless since it is too high, slow, and too easy to volley.

The Lob:

Singles: Seldom used, and then almost solely as a defensive time-saver, to allow a player to recover from an awkward position.

Doubles: The soundest defense shot in the game. Used to break up team work and to force a team away from the net. This shot may be considered one of the most important of all strokes in doubles.

The Volley:

Singles: Used whenever the opportunity offers, but is the completion of a ground stroke attack rather than the attack itself.

Doubles: It is the foundation of attack, the goal which every doubles team struggles to attain. The slogan of doubles is "volley whenever and however possible." No player can be a great doubles player without a great volley. The volley in singles is valuable but not absolutely essential; but in doubles it is fundamentally a necessity.

The Smash:

Singles: A valuable point winner, seldom used, because the lob is so seldom employed.

Doubles: The crowning glory of a great doubles team, the weapon to crush in the lobbing defense which most doubles team use. The smash in doubles must carry more speed, direction and decision than singles because it must beat two men, not one. The overhead can never be more valuable than the lobbing used by the other team, because only off a lob can an overhead be used.

The Lob-Volley:

There is one shot that is peculiar to doubles and one of the most skillful and valuable in the game. It is the lob-volley. This shot is played from the volleying-position at the net and should be made when both teams are drawn into close quarters battling for position. It is seldom played, in fact its value is hardly recognized. The shot wins by virtue of its surprise on the opponents, its ability to catch them off balance, and its inherent soundness. It is nothing more than a toss from a volley rather than a hit. It should be about ten feet high and slow, with a little undercut spin. There are a few American players who use it, notably Johnston, Richards, and at times Williams; but what is significant is its inclusion in the games of several youngsters, notably Arnold Jones, George Lott and Sandy Wiener. It shows the shot is gaining in popularity and will shortly be in the repertory of every good doubles player.

One reason the doubles game requires so much finesse and subtlety is the fact that you must outguess two minds, not one. In the

United States the ideal doubles team, in the popular mind, are two men of equal strength and the same type game, playing equal portions of the court, usually divided by the center service line extended indefinitely. If either man crosses the line into his partner's court, the American idea is outraged and the team "has no team work." I know of nothing more ridiculous than this theory. Watch all the great European or Australian teams and you will find that both men play all over the court, the criterion of their team work resting on the results obtained. I have always felt doubles was a game to win, not to work out theoretical divisions of team play on the court. It makes no difference which man makes the kill so long as it is made and the point won. The only crime in "poaching" is not to end the point. If you "poach," at least finish your shot, either with a winner or an error.

Let me explain just what my ideal doubles combination can do. Each player has the ability and willingness to both defend the ball and to kill it. On any given point one may or should defend and attempt to make an opening for his partner to make the kill. Should the opposing attack switch, then this defense can switch. If, at any moment, either man sees a kill, even though it must be made on his partner's sideline and his partner cannot reach it in time to kill, I say that man should cross over and kill.

Patience and co-operation are the keynote of doubles success. It is useless to attempt to play with a partner in whom one lacks confidence or with whom one has no desire to play. I cannot make claims to any authority as a doubles player, in fact I have been considered for years to be one of the worst doubles players among the top flight men. I admit all that, yet I believe that my theory of doubles, that of defense, finesse and the willingness to poach, if developed by a man who understands doubles, is far superior to the modern American idea. Gerald Patterson and Pat O'Hara Wood, in team work, carry out my idea of perfect doubles. It is only in their errors of racquet technique, not in strategy or position, that they meet defeat. I believe that errors should be cut down to the minimum in doubles. They are bad enough in singles, but they are fatal in doubles.

I stress the value of putting your service in, and, above all, putting the ball in play off service. The outstanding fault with the doubles teams of the United States, in marked contrast to those of Europe or Australia, is their inability, or rather unwillingness, to put the ball in play off service. They are not willing to defend their first return, but insist on attempting to win outright, with the result that they make four errors to one placement. There is the desire to batter down a defense rather than to undermine and finally demolish it by gradual disintegration. The battering process is splendid if you can hold the attack, but in a great majority of cases the number of errors far exceed the earned points. One reason Williams and Washburn have not quite reached the top flight, the

Championship itself, is because their defense is not equal to their attack. They will have a streak for a set or two, when their attack is going just right, when they sweep all before them, yet it wabbles and they have no sound defense to back it up. One reason for the success of such teams as Hackett and Alexander, Ward and Wright, and Johnston and Griffin, lies in the patience and steadiness of their defense, with which they bolstered their attack. Over-anxiety seldom leads them into disastrous errors. Costly errors have lost more tennis matches than earned points have ever won.

If the United States is to attain the position in doubles which we hold in singles we must recognize our deficiencies and overcome them. We must place greater stress on the value of the return of service. We must be willing to recognize the value of poaching and its absolute necessity in first-class doubles. We must develop teams that can play the Australian formation with the partner of the receiver at the net to volley the server's volley, a method beautifully illustrated in the play of Pat O'Hara Wood and Gerald Patterson, or in the marvelous anticipation of Norman E. Brookes, the greatest doubles player of all time.

In other words, we must come out of the doubles nursery and learn the real doubles game.

CHAPTER VI

THE ALL-COURT GAME

MODERN tennis is the equilibrium of the pendulum after two long swings. It is the sound, sane, sensible combination of the best tennis of all periods.

The original growth of tennis produced the baseline driver. The outstanding figures of that period, which stretched over two and a half decades, included such outstanding driving stars as S. H. Smith and A. W. Gore of England, R. D. Sears, Harry Slocum, on through even to the transition period which culminated in our greatest baseliner, William A. Larned. It was during the last dozen years of this period, which ended about 1911, that experimental minds in the game were working along the lines of the net attack. Malcolm Whitman, the Wrenns, and notably Holcombe Ward, Beals Wright and William Clothier were meeting with success by advancing to the net whenever possible. The game was still essentially baseline driving, with the cry "depth" as its slogan. Anyone who drove within less than five feet of the baseline was looked upon as hardly worthy of consideration, yet speed as we understand it today, blinding, battering, crushing, was unknown. Larned had "pace," momentum, to his shots, yet where was there a shot of the type of Johnston's or Anderson's forehand wallop?

Then came the miracle, that lop-sided game as far on the side of speed and net attack as it had been conservatively on the baseline previously. It was Maurice Mc-Loughlin, he of the red hair, gleaming smile and pulverizing punch in service and smash. He swept the country. He revolutionized the game. During the years 1912, 1913 and 1914 when McLoughlin was in his prime, speed ran rampant through the tennis world. Everywhere players discarded their ground games to adopt a fast service and a smashing net attack. Safety was an unknown word in

CHARLES S. GARLAND
United States
Forest Hills, 1919

A characteristic position and shot of a player who at nineteen became an Internationalist and member of the 1920 Davis Cup team that won from British Isles. With R. N. Williams, 2nd, "Chuck" Garland won the English Doubles Championship at Wimbledon, beating Tilden and Johnston in five sets.

PLATE 27

THE BOUNDING BASQUE BOUNDS

Jean Borotra leaps in to volley. Apparently his opponent's shot must have hit the net, but Borotra in his eagerness seems destined to plunge over the barrier. An example of over-play and over-anxiety.

PLATE 28

the tennis game in the United States. The god Speed was at the wheel, driving the game on to danger.

Then came another reaction, exemplified in the person of Richard Norris Williams, 2nd. This young American, recently returned from his studies abroad, his tennis obviously influenced by the modern trend of the rising bounce style of the European game, had been pressing McLoughlin closely, until in 1914 he swept the great Californian into the discard. Williams, with the characteristic daring of his youth and natural love of the unexpected, had carried the European style about two steps further in and played every ground stroke off the rising bounce. Williams was essentially a baseliner, but a baseliner who played two feet inside the baseline instead of ten feet behind it like the old stars.

Moreover, Williams combined a speedy service and an aggressive net attack with his foundation of the ground game. He was the connecting link between the passing style and the one to come.

It was during this period, say from 1907 to 1914, that one figure appeared who in my opinion was nearly ten years ahead of his time. This man was Norman E. Brookes, the Australian wizard. When other players knew nothing of the all-court game Brookes was playing and studying it with a certainty and knowledge which we today may well be proud to some day attain. It was Brookes who, even with a somewhat unsound ground stroke equipment, developed the perfect balance of the two styles in actual match play. Even today, in 1924, Brookes is experimenting with and working along the lines of new shots for the future game. Brookes was our first real all-court player.

Williams was a disciple of speed like McLoughlin, only his speed was off the ground, while the Californian's was from the net; yet in each case the influence was toward over-offense rather than sound defense.

It was 1915 that saw the first national

The All-Court Game

Championship rest on the brow of a man who was destined to point the way to the modern, sane, and to my way of thinking, correct game of today. William M. Johnston, also a Californian, swept to victory in 1915, beating both Williams and McLoughlin by the solid, sound, defense and the powerful punching offense of his all-court game. The period from 1912 to 1917, when the World War put a period to sport, was one of change and uncertainty, with Johnston the rising figure by virtue of his all-court style, Williams slipping slightly, while McLoughlin faded from the picture.

Then came the close of the World War and with it the revival of sports, particularly tennis, the world over. New figures had risen during the few years while others had passed on. The most notable sacrifice from the tennis game was Anthony F. Wilding, a loss which can never be replaced, for in game and sportsmanship Wilding stood a model. I have said little or nothing about Wilding in my book because I never saw him play and never met him. It is difficult enough to do justice to genius when it is personally encountered, but to attempt to do so where it is not personally met is impossible, so I can but add my word of sorrowful regret at Wilding's passing and write on of others whom I know.

Since the war new all-court stars have gained prominence. A new era seems even now peeping around the corner at the all-court game. Vincent Richards, Henri Cochet, Rene Lacoste, Manuel Alonso and Brian I. C. Norton are the most notable examples of the all-court game, plus something new.

It was during the years from 1916 to 1920 that I was gradually gaining mastery of my varied strokes and proving, what I had always contended, against great opposition— that no player can have too many strokes in his equipment. Even as a boy I was a believer in the varied, all-court game, yet during the years I was experimenting with the different strokes I was told repeatedly and

AN INTERNATIONAL MIXED DOUBLES TEAM

On the Centre Court at Wimbledon in 1922 Mlle. Suzanne Lenglen and Pat O'Hara Wood are playing Mrs. Molla Bjurstedt Mallory and Dean Mathey. The tremendous speed and aggressiveness of Mlle. Lenglen are shown in a striking manner.

PLATE 29

A STRANGE DOUBLES POSITION

Henri Cochet crosses in front of Jean Borotra for a certain kill of a short lob. Cochet, sensing the fact Borotra was too deep, came across for the kill. This is one reason Continental doubles team are better than those of the U. S. A.—because they are not afraid to poach on their partner.

PLATE 30

vehemently that I was crazy, that I was
working along the wrong idea, that I should
concentrate on one style and play it, that I
could never learn to both drive and chop,
that, all in all, I was a typical dub. For
years this last estimate appeared correct,
for I was indiscriminately and monotonously
defeated. Finally the turn came, and with
the years since the war I have trod the up-
path.

What is this all-court game? What does
it include? First, I claim it must include *all*
the standard strokes; service, both slice and
twist; drive and chop, both fore- and backhand, volley and smash. Second, it must include varied depth. No longer will consistently deep driving prove a satisfactory standard. Today one must vary distance as well
as direction. The short shot has its place in
modern tennis just as much as the deep one.
Third, the all-court game demands varied
spin of the ball, with which to change pace.
Every player must be able to both under-cut
and top-spin his ground shots. Fourth, there

109

must be *controlled* speed. Please note the word "controlled." Speed alone will not suffice; it must include sufficient control to vary it according to the opponent you face.

If I were to attempt to define the all-court game tersely, I should call it "consistent-inconsistency." In other words, you must be able to vary your game at will, both as to direction and depth, speed and spin.

What is the future of the tennis game? Have we reached the ultimate development of the game in the champions of the present? Many critics believe we have. Personally I say we have not. I say it without equivocation and with authority. As one of the champions of today, I see vistas of progress ahead, of which I glimpse only a bit, but which the champions of tomorrow will have explored and developed. Where are these lanes of progress? Not from the backcourt, for the great players of the past have found all there is to find from there.

Not from the net, for McLoughlin, Murray, Church, etc., have explored the volley and smash to its limit. It is rather in the use of the forecourt for sharp-angled passing shots, in the use of the mid-court volley, the half volley and rising bounce shots, that future progress lies. Watch Richards, Cochet, Lacoste, and many of the younger players, and you will see signs of new shots, or attempts at new shots, along these lines of progress that point the way to the future.

Every player who desires to succeed in the future must equip himself with every shot in tennis and then strive to explore the mysteries of the forecourt. Yet at this time, when I am speaking of the last word in tennis technique, the ultimate in stroke production, let me for a moment sound the warning that on the rock of first principles the new game must be built. You cannot learn the fine points without complete mastery of the fundamentals. Most players slur over the importance of that cardinal point, without which modern tennis, in fact any tennis, is impossible.

111

Keep your eye on the Ball
and
Keep your mind on the Game.

It is impossible to overstress these points. Fully 95 per cent of errors are due either to not watching the ball, or to lack of attention to your stroke at the moment of making it. The greater the diversity of stroke, the more varied the spin, speed and direction of a player's game, the greater the chance of error, and therefore the more important that he should keep his eye on the ball. Any player may learn strokes if he has mastered the secret of watching the ball, but the greatest stroke player in the world will go down to defeat if he allows himself to grow careless in the fundamentals of the game.

The future lies ahead with its tantalizing glimpses of unexplored roads of progress.

Would that I were not an old dog who finds it hard to learn new tricks, for I would gladly attempt to explore some of these roads. In fact, I may try it anyway. The young stars have their chance. To them I say, go

TWO PLAYERS FROM THE BRITISH ISLES

James Cecil Parke (at right) who came to America in 1908, 1909 and 1914, and whose defeat of Norman Brookes in Australia in 1912 amazed the world. At the left is Algernon R. F. Kingscote, whose five set match with William T. Tilden, 2nd, at Wimbledon in 1920, was the most critical one for the latter.

PLATE 31

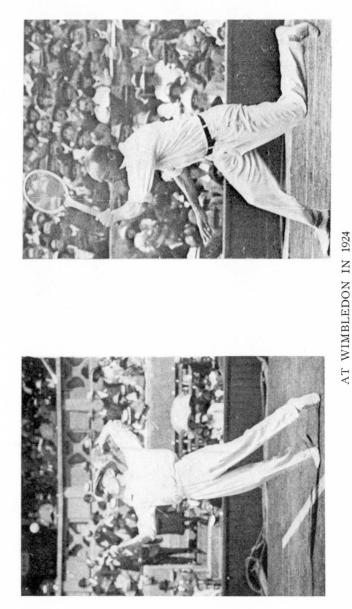

AT WIMBLEDON IN 1924

Norman E. Brookes (at left) serving to Francis T. Hunter. Jean Washer, who defeated Brookes the next day.

PLATE 32

AN INTERNATIONAL PAIR OF ACES

Forest Hills, 1924

William M. Johnston (U. S. A.) and Jean Rene Lacoste (France) just
before the match in the 1924 U. S. Championship which Johnston won
after a brilliant display by both men.

PLATE 33

A STUDY IN CONTRASTING STYLES

Gerald L. Patterson (at left) hits a forehand drive in the peculiar cramped style that marks some of his shots. Ichiya Kumagae is shown at the completion of his forehand "loop drive". Note his faulty footwork, with the weight travelling away from the shot; and the peculiar grip.

Plate 34

out into the highways and byways of the game and bring back, developed, those interesting but imperfect shots that today lie on the edge of our modern tennis in its all-court games.

Chapter VII

THE VALUE OF INTENSIVE PRACTICE

ONE becomes very weary of copy book epigrams in the days of one's youth, because they drive down one's throat many true but uninteresting (at the moment) facts. We have all written many hundred copies of the good old standby, "Practice makes perfect." One does not need to become actually antique to discover that nothing, not even practice, makes anything, or anyone, perfect.

Yet hidden in the dear old fossil of a copybook bromide is a bit of sound tennis advice. Practice may not make perfect, but believe me it has made many a good tennis player. I am a great believer in practice, but above all in intensive practice. My idea of intensive practice is to pick out one stroke and hammer away at that shot until it is completely mastered. This is the system I have used with marked success in working with Sandy Wiener and Donald Strachan.

My greatest success with the system was the development of my own backhand from a feeble defense chop to an offensive attacking drive, through the intensive practice of one Winter and at the cost of many lickings. Any player who seriously dislikes to accept defeat should never try intensive practice on one stroke.

My backhand was born in the Winter of 1919-20. Its place of birth was Providence, Rhode Island. Its godfathers, fosterfathers and various other sorts of parents were J. D. E. Jones, his son Arnold W. Jones, Russell Dana and several others. Its chief victim was myself. My backhand reached this earth through the fact that the United States challenged for the Davis Cup in 1920 and the Davis Cup Committee indicated to me that I would be considered seriously for the team that Summer. Up to and including 1919, my backhand had been a shining mark at which anyone could plug away with impunity. Billy Johnston had smeared it to a pulp in the final round of The Championship in 1919, at which time he annexed three sets while I was still seeking one. The many errors off my backhand lived clearly in my memory, and when the announcement of the challenge for the Davis Cup was made public, and it was intimated to me that I might go abroad with the team, I determined that if I went I would leave my old backhand in the United States and take a new one with me.

It is no easy job to learn a new stroke in three or four months, particularly when it is a new trick for an old dog, yet it had to be done. My first step was to work out a sound grip, swing and footwork, not a very difficult thing to do in theory, and, once worked out, to put it in practice. There came the amusement for every one but me. Four times a week, sometimes more often, Mr. Jones, or Arnold and I would do battle in the indoor court which Jones owns in Providence.

I set out to learn a backhand and every

JOHN HENNESSEY
United States
Forest Hills, 1924

This young player from Indianapolis was the sensation of the 1924 season, culminating in his win from Jean Borotra, the Wimbledon Champion, in a bitterly fought five set match in The Championship. Hennessey is seen making his peculiar backhand "loop" shot.

PLATE 35

GEORGE M. LOTT, Jr.
United States
Forest Hills, 1924

National Junior Champion, 1923 and 1924, at the completion of his tremendous forehand drive.

PLATE 36

shot I could play backhand I played. I intended to learn a drive, and drive I did. Only the walls or the net could stop my efforts during the first weeks. Far and wide went my shots, yet even at the darkest moments, when I was ready to burn my racquets and quit the game—and these moments were not infrequent—I would make one beautiful shot once in a long while that gave me courage to go on. It would prove by its very effectiveness that I was on the right road, and that only the mastery of the mechanics of the stroke stood between me and my new backhand. Week by week I saw my backhand grow. Sometimes I would think I had lost it; the touch would go for days at a time and I could not hit the ball in the court; then back it would come again, better than before.

Over these weeks my pride suffered many a humiliation. It is not particularly enjoyable to a Davis Cup candidate to be repeatedly defeated by either a junior or a veteran who had virtually retired from active tennis some years before. Many a defeat at the hands of both I swallowed and laid them, often not too silently, on the altar of my backhand drive. Gradually the turn came. I began to gain control of the new shot. It seemed to me that, in a period of about ten days, the work of the whole winter crystallized and my game jumped ahead a full class. I played better tennis, in certain ways, than I had ever played before in all my life.

It is true that certain other shots suffered by this concentration on the backhand drive, but they came back quickly because I had the foundation for them. I had held myself steadily to hitting my backhand *hard,* and I found that this steady punch had a tendency to speed up my entire game. I was gaining in aggressive tactics.

One cannot work consistently on anything without obtaining definite and interesting results. The only drawback is the length of time it takes to show these results. Most players are not willing to devote more than a week or two at the most to the mastery of a stroke. If they have not the desired result then they usually let it go with a shrug. "What is the use?" they say. Well, possibly they are right; yet it seems a shame to me to pass up the ability to do anything well, simply because the effort seems tedious. Strokes cannot be learned in weeks, they must be reckoned in months, and actual progress in years.

I have never regretted the hours, days and weeks that I spent to acquire my backhand drive, for to it, and it primarily, I lay my United States and World's Championship titles. I am convinced that had I not done the work necessary to the mastery of that stroke, Johnston would have continued to defeat me just as decisively after 1919 as he did that year.

I do not mean that 1920 saw my backhand drive complete. Far from it. I worked and am still working on it, as on all my strokes, for they all can stand development. The daily practice Johnston and I had against each other in New Zealand in 1920-21 was

119

largely responsible for the solidification of my game, yet all the tennis I have played would not have produced that backhand drive if I had not put in the period of constructive, intensive training in 1920 in the Indoor court in Providence.

Accidents sometimes prove a blessing in disguise. One could hardly recommend the loss of a finger as a definite asset to a tennis player, nor yet as the most ideal method of training. Yet, strange as it sounds, I owe a marked improvement in my net game, volley and smash to the accident of the loss of my middle finger of my right hand. I had been too soft in my volley game and overhead. I always knew that, yet somehow or other, in the days when I had all my fingers, I never could drive myself to kill.

In 1922 I met Sandy Wiener, and the boy and I started to play doubles together. Then, late that year, came my accident and the resultant loss of my finger and what, for a time, seemed to be the end of my tennis. Finally, with the Spring of 1923, I began my attempt

120

KIRK M. REID
United States
Forest Hills, 1924

The forehand drive of the former Cornell captain, whose defeat of Pat O'Hara Wood in the 1924 Championship, in a five set match, was one of the surprises of the meeting.

PLATE 37

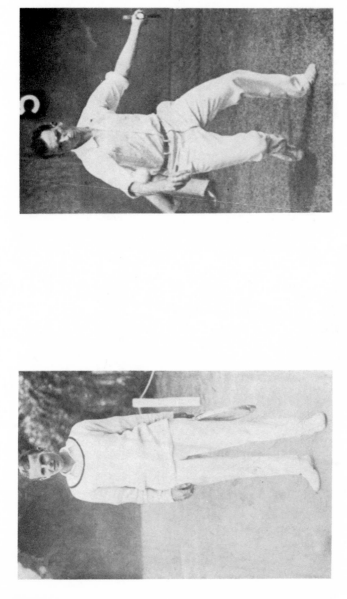

TWO YOUNG AMERICAN PLAYERS

At left is Emmett Pare of Chicago, who has a sound, all-court game and combines with it coolness, courage and resource. At right is Wallace Scott of Washington State, 1924 Intercollegiate champion, who is seen making a forehand drive.

Plate 38

to come back. I quickly discovered that certain soft shots of finesse that I had formerly relied upon at the net were gone from my game forever. Sandy and I were once more playing doubles, but my lack of finishing shots had us in trouble, since the boy was then too young to play on even terms with the rest in fast company, a condition which he remedied in 1924, when he jumped far up the tennis ladder. I discovered that either I must learn to volley decisively and smash to kill, or Sandy and I would meet far more defeats than pleased either of us.

Once more I found myself facing intensive practice, this time from necessity. All through the season of 1923 I pounded away at my volley and overhead. Naturally, I found the loss of my finger had affected my grip on the racquet and that it turned in my hand quite often. This increased the need for a speedy win of a point. I could no longer rely on my ability to outsteady my opponent. I must hit for a winner at once. Gradually my incessant "punching" of volleys and overheads began to pay dividends. I actually reached a point when I was reasonably certain of winning at the net. I gained confidence, and with my confidence grew my effectiveness. I have always felt that the keynote of success against Johnston in the finals of 1923—and partially so in 1924—was the fact that on crucial points, when I advanced to the net, I could win outright by volley or smash if I could place my racquet on the ball at all.

I feel that I owe my improved volley and overhead to Sandy Wiener and to the loss of my finger. I will never be a great volleyer and smasher. I know that. I have not the genius for the net game that characterizes Vincent Richards or Bill Johnston. They are my superiors in every department of the volley and smash, but at least my intensive practice, so unusually forced upon me, raised my volley game to new heights.

There seems much of conceit in this chapter of personal progress. I do not mean it as such. It is the lesson to be learned from

122

these two steps up the tennis ladder that is my excuse for their inclusion in this book. What I did, with this degree of success, many other players with far greater natural talent than I, and there are many, for I am a hand-made tennis player, can do with better effect and in less time. Intensive practice over a period of some weeks will fill many a gap in the game of players who today are plough-ing through the disheartening period of the "almost-great." Intensive practice for three months could give Vincent Richards a drive off his forehand and backhand. Intensive practice should teach Howard Kinsey to hit hard off the ground. Gerald Patterson, fol-lowing the 1924 Davis Cup season, told me he was returning to Australia to practice his backhand and footwork; and if successful in his attempt to bolster his weaknesses he would return to the United States in 1925.

There are many players who are handi-capped by some glaring hole in their game which, unless remedied, will always chain them to the second flight. The day of the player with a lop-sided game is over. Today the Champion cannot afford to show weakness. Tomorrow, he must have even greater strength. The boys like Emmett Pare, Sandy Wiener, Donald Strachan, Howard Langlie, Horace Orser, Kenneth Appel and many others, who are learning every shot in the game while yet juniors, will go further as men than the boys like George Lott, who rely upon a freak game plus sheer force to carry them to victory.

If there is a hole in your game, plug it by intensive practice. Do not worry about the defeats you must bear during the time your game is developing. Go out to make of yourself the greatest player that lies within the range of your natural abilities and your opportunities.

Sometimes a player is called upon to face a serious problem, when, too late, after habits of poor stroke productions are formed, he finds himself face to face with the question of his future development. If he continues his old methods, he has little or no real future in the game. He may make the First Ten, or he may not; but he will never be a serious aspirant for Championship honors. On the other hand, if he discards his old style and sets out to learn a new, sound one, he runs the danger of ruining his old game and never mastering his new one. He takes a gamble on the possible Championship against tennis oblivion. It is a serious problem.

John Hennessey of Indianapolis, who startled the tennis world in 1924 by his defeats of Patterson, Norton, Harada and Borotra, was called upon to face it. Hennessey was twenty-four years old, and he had played enough tennis in his life to be considered a well-seasoned player. He is a fine natural athlete, a fighter, equipped with a good forehand, a reliable service, volley and overhead, but handicapped with a very unsound and unorthodox slice backhand which, during 1924, he attempted to bolster up with a peculiar "wrist-flick," topped drive, even more unsound. Hennessey, with his old game

125

intact, stood certain of the First Ten but equally certain never to win the Championship title unless he plugged the hole in his game. He had had three conclusive proofs of this fact, once at the hands of Wallace Johnson and twice from me. I cannot say at the time of writing exactly what road Hennessey will take. I believe he will turn to intensive practice on the backhand and gamble his game against his chance for the Championship. I hope he does. I know I would in his place. I hope success crowns his effort. Time, and time alone, can tell. Let us watch Hennessey in the years to come.

Sometimes a word of advice at the right moment, even if it seems unnecessarily severe, will start a player on the road to progress. I had an interesting example of that in Chicago last Spring. Emmett Pare, the young Chicago boy who proved himself the sensation of the 1924 junior season, is a great friend of mine, and during a short trip to the Windy City in May I managed to find time to play a few sets with him. He impressed me as careless and inclined to be a trifle self-satisfied from his successes the previous year. I did not hesitate to tell him my views, in which I was supported by Pare's staunch supporter, Walter Hayes, and by S. Wallis Merrihew, editor of AMERICAN LAWN TENNIS. We pointed out in no uncertain terms the dangers of over-confidence; we picked his game to pieces, dissecting his backhand for particular examination and condemnation. Emmett listened with interest, said little and went to work. Within the short space of three months, when next I saw him, he had developed a real backhand, was once more the fighting, hardworking kid I had known and, today, seems headed for the Championship heights.

Those few words of sound advice saved a great player. We are not the ones who deserve credit for it, but Pare himself, for he saw the truth in them and by determination and intensive practice yanked himself from the rut into which he had allowed himself to fall, and set his feet firmly on the road to success.

Plug the holes in your game! There is far more pleasure to tennis if you have no fear about your strokes. There is no sensation more thrilling than the impact of the ball on the strings of a racquet as a perfect stroke turns it back against your opponent.

CHAPTER VIII.

YOUTH TO THE FORE

EVERY season that passes makes the path harder for the veteran. Some of us who are now "veteran internationalists" and verging on the place where we must admit to the doubtful title of "aged net star," find our roads blocked by new and better young players every season.

Seldom has any one year found the "dope" spilled so consistently as 1924, and in almost every case the upset was furnished by a youngster. European tennis was dominated by the sensational performances of the trio of young French stars, Jean Borotra, Rene Lacoste, and Henri Cochet, all of whom were less than twenty-five. There is another time and place in this book to speak of them. My present task is to deal with the rising stars of the United States. Certainly there is a wealth of talent from which to draw my subjects. Young players were rampant from New York to California, Canada to Mexico. Dozens of them spilled the struggling veterans along the tournament track.

I must accord the place of honor for the 1924 season to John Hennessey of Indianapolis. True, Vincent Richards was at his best but Richards, for all his twenty-one years, is a "veteran internationalist" and his tribute must come elsewhere. Hennessey, an almost unknown, annexed the scalps of more visiting Davis Cup players than any other one man in the United States. He started his repelling of the foreign invasion when he placed B. I. C. "Babe" Norton in the discard in the Western Championship. Not satisfied with this, on the following day Hennessey quietly eliminated Gerald L. Patterson, the Australian Davis Cup captain, from the same event. Then he took a rest for some weeks, until the National Singles, when, on successive days, he defeated Harada of Japan, Kong of China (orientals were his specialty) and then Borotra of France. It was no flash

in the pan for Hennessey, but the result of
serious consistent tennis of a very high order.
His advance to the front rank of American
tennis is well deserved. John Hennessey is a
pleasing modest personality, meeting victory
or defeat with a grin that endears him to
public and players alike. He will be a real
asset to the game.

Second only to Hennessey in their meteoric
rise are George M. Lott, Jr., of Chicago and
Alfred H. Chapin, Jr., of Springfield, Mass.
Lott, National Junior Champion, 1923 and
1924, advanced by leaps and bounds during
the last season. He reached the position of
premier player of Chicago, ranking Walter
Hayes and Lucien Williams. In the 1924
National Championship he eliminated R. N.
Williams, 2nd, and Chapin, Jr., and reached
the last eight, where Gerald Patterson put
him out. It is a peculiar game which Lott
has developed. It has superlative features
in the tremendous speed of his forehand, his
sound decisive volleying and overhead; yet
it is lop-sided, for his backhand is erratic and

his service none too reliable. I cannot say I consider Lott's game sound. He is a good match player except when his temperament overcomes him and he falls a victim to himself. He has courage and fighting spirit, at times almost too much of the latter.

Alfred H. Chapin is another young player whose 1924 season placed him very near the first flight. "Chape's" strokes are sound, far sounder in style than those of Lott or Hennessey. He has no serious weakness, like the backhands of the other two, but he lacks the tenacity of purpose and ability to carry on that characterizes Lott. There is very little to choose between these three young stars. I should say that Hennessey is the best today, that Lott is the most dangerous and that Chapin has the soundest game for future development.

Kirk Reid, of Cleveland, with a victory over Pat O'Hara Wood in The Championship and a close match with Howard Kinsey, is another young star who forged ahead in 1924. Reid, once runner-up in the Intercollegiate Championship (in 1919) where he carried Charles S. Garland to five sets, has at last succeeded in steadying his erratic wildness and flattening a game that is still almost too full of overtopped drives.

Cincinnati has a promising player in Louis Kuhler, a player with beautiful strokes, well produced, but a player who is prone to over-hit at all times. If Kuhler can learn to combine brains with brawn in his stroke equipment he may go far in the near future. He has few technical weaknesses and no glaring faults.

The colleges are annually producing scores of promising young players. One reason for this is the great increase in interest in tennis in the high and preparatory schools that feed the colleges, as well as increased interest in the sport in the colleges themselves. The 1924 Intercollegiate title journeyed to the Pacific Northwest when Wallace Scott of Washington University annexed the singles. Scott is a most interesting player, crude but potentially dangerous and capable of fine things. His game at present is almost an echo of Maurice McLoughlin in tactics if not in execution. It is a tremendous, crushing, blinding service, followed to the net for a kill. Scott has not the sound development of many of the other young stars but he has dynamic energy and abounding vitality that wins for him today.

Arnold W. Jones, of Yale, almost fulfilled the promise he gave as National Junior Champion. Jones, with his glorious forehand, improving backhand and splendid volleying, is once more one of the most promising prospects for the future. He has emerged from his slump of 1923, and only a long trip abroad in 1924 accounts for him not having joined Chapin, Lott and Hennessey as one of the outstanding figures of the year.

William W. Ingraham of Harvard is another player whose absence abroad as a member of the Harvard-Yale team, of which Jones was also a member, is the reason for his apparent retrogression. Actually Ingraham played fine tennis in 1924 during the short time he was in the United States. He has a well conceived, but too soft, game, one that needs more speed before he will scale the heights. He is a marvelous defensive player and one of the most remarkable defensive volleyers I have ever seen, but he lacks the winning punch.

Frank T. Anderson of Columbia, undoubtedly one of the finest young stars in America, was the unfortunate victim of illness that put him out of competition for the greater portion of the 1924 season. I understand his health will permit his return in 1925, and his fine, all-court game should once more carry him well up the ladder.

Lewis White and Louis Thalheimer of Texas, the Intercollegiate Doubles Champions, are a pair of youngsters who show great promise. White is slightly the sounder of the two but Thalheimer has flights of very fine tennis. Both boys have well rounded games, with splendidly grounded form and few weaknesses. I am inclined to believe one or both of them may be among the top flight in the near future.

California, as always, has a large group of fine young stars coming to the fore. Cranston Holman of San Francisco, runner-up to George Lott in the National, shows a well rounded game that has all the earmarks of future greatness. Holman is not as severe as many of the Californians, but I should say sounder. Philip Bettins is still a promising young star but his development has not been as rapid and sound as I had expected. His service is splendid, and his forehand and volleying are always dangerous, but he is afflicted with the bugbear of so many players, a weak backhand. He has done little or nothing to improve this defect or remedy it during the past two years. Elmer Griffin, brother to Clarence J., gave a splendid account of himself in the 1924 National Singles by his defeat of Okamoto of the Japanese Davis Cup team. He showed a crafty subtle game, not unlike that of Peck.

There are so many good young players in

MLLE. SUZANNE LENGLEN IN 1923

The World's Champion on grass retained her title at Wimbledon
by a big margin. The picture tells eloquently of the speed and
aggressiveness of the French player.

Plate 39

MISS HELEN NEWINGTON WILLS
United States
Forest Hills, 1924

An excellent photo of the Champion's backhand drive, which is that rare thing, a *forcing* backhand. Note the position of body and feet and the close watch of the oncoming ball.

PLATE 40

California one cannot do justice to all. Alan Herrington of Los Angeles impressed me with the improvement in his style between 1923 and 1924. I believe that Herrington has real possibilities in his game, because he combines good strokes with a keen, experimental, studious attitude to the game.

A young star who created quite a sensation was Fritz Mercur of Lehigh University. His great victory was won at the Longwood Cricket Club, where he succeeded in placing his name on the famous bowl. He defeated Nat W. Niles, Wallace Johnson and L. B. Rice, a splendid performance. Mercur seems to have recovered from his old flights of erraticness, due to his desire to kill every shot. He has sound strokes which this year he uses with excellent judgment so that we may expect to see Mercur advance steadily in coming seasons.

There are many other players who deserve mention but I have not the knowledge or the space. In collegiate ranks one may pay special attention to Jerry Lang, Ed Chandler and Charles Watson III.

In the ranks of the younger juniors and boys there are so many promising youngsters I hardly know where to begin or whom to mention. I have already spoken of George Lott, the National Junior title holder and several other juniors. New York boasts a boy who has all the earmarks of a great player, in the person of Horace Orser. If ever there was an absolute double of a tennis game, Orser is the double of Vincent Richards; yet, strange to say, although Orser knows Richards casually, he has played very little with him. Orser has the same peculiar ground game, based on the slice, as Richards. I think his forehand is slightly sounder in form than Vinnie's, while his backhand is a replica. The same natural gift of volleying, the perfect wrist work, the marvelous balance and weight control that have always distinguished Richards, are the gift of the gods to Horace Orser. He even follows the line of duplication to the point of delivery of service, which, like Richards, is his weakest point.

Orser's closest rival in the junior ranks around New York is Kenneth Appel, a hard hitting, sensational youngster, whose game is at least as sound as Orser, but who seems to lack that intuitive tennis sense that distinguishes Orser at all times. Appel has a tremendous service, a splendid aggressive forehand, a reliable sound backhand and a good net game that should produce better results than he has yet obtained. Stuart Gayness, George Agutter's pupil, is another metropolitan star with sound shots but a depressing inability to master his game at critical times. Gayness is an uncertain quantity, who may suddenly find himself and jump to a place of national fame or who may sink into tennis oblivion in a few years.

The O'Loughlan boys, Dave, John, and little Billy, the Johnstown trio, are a family who may produce at least one Champion. All these youngsters have sound all-court games. 1924 was a disastrous year for Dave, who up to then had been marching forward steadily, from his first year in the game until he held the Boys' National Championship in 1922. I must mention at this place the sensation of the 1924 junior season although I deal with him at greater length elsewhere. He is Emmett Pare of Chicago and, in my opinion, the first great natural player the Middle West has produced in over a decade. Watch Pare in the coming years. He seems destined for mighty works.

Philadelphia has a trio of very promising youngsters at the Germantown Cricket Club in Neil J. Sullivan, A. L. (Sandy) Wiener and Donald Strachan. These three boys are as fine examples of all-court technique as can be found in the junior ranks.

Seattle, far in the Pacific Northwest, already proud of her group of young stars which included Marshall Allen and Armand Marion, has sent another wonderful prospect East in the person of Howard Langlie. This youngster has all the shots in tennis, executed with a dash and vigor that spells future victory if today they cost him defeats. He is a tennis diamond, still in the rough, brilliant but in need of polishing.

Malcolm Hill and Harry C. Johnston lead the Boston district, both boys proving themselves splendid stroke players with few weaknesses. Little C. Alphonse Smith, Jr., of Annapolis, who won the National Boys' title in 1924, is, at last, a splendidly equipped young player. When I first knew young Smith, in 1922 and 1923, he had nothing but a chop stroke and all kinds of courage, but 1924 saw him blossom out with a new and excellent forehand drive, and also a real volley game which carried him to the championship of his class.

The most interesting and in many ways promising young boy that I have seen in years is Walter Thomas of Elizabeth, New Jersey. He is a pocket edition of Billy Johnston. He packs a wicked wallop in his forehand, volleys well, is deadly overhead for a kid and serves well. His only weakness, other than size, is his backhand, which

141

is now steadily improving. I look to see Walter Thomas go far in the tennis world.

Indianapolis, with Julius Sagalowski and Leo Kurzrock, has a pair of juniors from which to make a Champion to assist John Hennessey. I look more to Kurzrock than Sagalowski, for "Sag" has slipped a little in 1924.

I cannot begin to do justice to the thousands of promising boys playing the game. I have passed over dozens who warrant a word quite as much as some I have included, but at the moment their names slip my memory. Watch the stars of the future emerge from the group I have mentioned, and quite possibly from some I have not. Youth to the fore! It is a welcome sign of healthy progress, which we veterans should hail with the sense of pleasure that comes from the knowledge that our game will be carried on in safe hands by players who will be our superiors.

CHAPTER IX

WOMEN'S TENNIS

I KNOW of no single question in tennis that causes so much discussion, among both players and those who have no direct connection with the game, as the relative ability and skill of the best women and the best men. I have heard violent arguments arise over whether Suzanne Lenglen could beat Vincent Richards or Helen Wills play even with Billy Johnston. I have heard people with real intelligence, who should have known better, attempt to prove that the best women's tennis equals the top flight of men's. Nothing can be more ridiculous. There is no comparison. The best women and the best men are not in the same class, in fact not by many classes. There are probably over a hundred players among the men who could easily defeat Suzanne Lenglen or Helen Wills, almost by whatever score they desired. I know something of this because in 1921 in Paris, my second day off the boat, I played one set with Mlle. Lenglen, which I won, 6-0.

Helen Wills is played even by second string club players. These statements are not made to detract from the game of these girls, for in their class they are just as perfect artists of the racquet as are men like Johnston or Richards; but I say what I do to prove that physical limitations place an unsurmountable handicap on the woman, which no amount of technical proficiency can overcome. It is the difference between the speed of foot and shot in the man and the woman that is just the difference in the games. No woman can cover court fast enough or hit hard enough consistently to hold a man of equal skill on equal terms.

These basic facts having been conclusively proved over the entire period of the world's history, through some means or other, we can accept them at face value and go on to ask ourselves, since women cannot play men's

MISS KATHLEEN McKANE

England

Wimbledon, 1923

The Champion of All-England, 1924, hits her forehand drive. Note the closeness of her watch of the ball.

PLATE 41

MRS. MOLLA BJURSTEDT MALLORY
United States
Gipsey Club (England), 1923

The six-times American Champion, making her magnificent forehand drive, the shot that carried her to the Championship more times than any other woman.

PLATE 42

MISS MARY K. BROWNE
United States

National Champion, 1912-13-14, who in 1924 reached the semi-final of the
National Tennis and the final of the National Golf Championships, making
a forehand drive. Note the perfect stance and the concentration on the ball.

PLATE 43

AMERICA'S PREMIER DOUBLES TEAM

Wimbledon, 1924

Mrs. Hazel Hotchkiss Wightman watches Miss Helen Wills volley a high backhand. This team won the English Olympic and United States titles in one season.

PLATE 44

tennis as men play it, What is the ideal style for women to adopt?

I have very strong views on this subject. I am absolutely convinced there is only one sound game for a woman and that is the base-line game. It is my belief, and has been my experience, that the woman does not live who can go to the net with success through three sets and stand up under it. If she attempts this method she must win in two sets or not at all.

Consider for a moment Mrs. Hazel Hotch-kiss Wightman and Miss Mary K. Browne, the two finest volleyers the United States has produced among women. Neither of these women could quite cope with the solid driv-ing game of Mrs. Molla Bjurstedt Mallory in a big match where every ounce of energy must be expended. Both Mrs. Wightman and Miss Browne could force Mrs. Mallory to the limit, often winning the first set and reach striking distance of the match, but their condition would fail and Mrs. Mallory would win out. The old cry of lack of condition, due to long retirement, would be raised. There was some slight ground for the argument, but the real answer lay in the style of game played.

Consider the outstanding figures in women's tennis over a period of twenty-five years. All were either baseline players, solely or at least basically baseliners, with the exceptions of Mrs. Wightman and possibly Miss Browne. In the United States one finds Mrs. May Sutton Bundy, Mrs. Barger Wallach, Mrs. Louise Hammond Raymond, Mrs. Helen Homans McLean, Mrs. Wightman, Miss Browne, Mrs. Mallory and Miss Helen Wills.

England has produced Mrs. Lambert Chambers, Mrs. Larcombe, Mrs. Beamish (all three absolutely baseline exponents), and Miss Kathleen McKane and Miss Ryan, a rather all-court pair. France is represented by Mme. Billioutt (Mlle. Broquedies), Mme. Golding and Mlle. Lenglen, all of whom are essentially baseliners, as are Mlle. Vlasto, the Greek-French girl and Mlle. Alvarez, the

Spanish champion. There must be some sound reason in the fact that over a period of twenty-five years baseline play is consistently successful. There is a marked and interesting trend in the play of Mlle. Lenglen, Kathleen McKane and Helen Wills, undoubtedly the three outstanding figures of 1924. All these girls, while essentially baseline players, go to the net to end a point, once they have driven their opponent out of court.

It may surprise many tennis followers who are acquainted with Suzanne Lenglen only by the press pictures or the news reel, which usually depict her on one toe with the other far over her head, as she makes a sensational volley or overhead, to know that in singles Mlle. Lenglen is the most conservative of baseliners, relying on her mechanical perfection and uncanny accuracy to defeat her opponent. She seldom goes to the net in singles except for a certain kill. This is not quite so true of Helen Wills and Kitty McKane. These two young stars will often advance to the net behind a shot that, while

147

forcing, is not actually an opening. They both volley more decisively than Mlle. Lenglen.

My idea of the perfect game for a woman to learn is:

The forehand drive of Molla Mallory. The backhand drive of Helen Wills. The volley of Hazel Wightman. The overhead of Hazel Wightman. The chop of Elizabeth Ryan. The service of Suzanne Lenglen.

After this is learned settle back to use primarily the first two shots and bring out the others only in the pinch. In other words, the girl of today who aspires to Championship honors must base her game, attack and defense, on the drive, and trim it with the other shots. She can do well to study the success of Molla Mallory who, with the drive and a courageous fighting spirit, rose to hold the championship of the world itself and is today still one of the greatest players in the world.

California has led the way in women's tennis in the United States. Champions have been showered from the Golden State. Every year sees new and interesting young players come East. Only four years ago, in 1920, our National Champion, Helen Wills, made her first appearance in the East, a school girl with pigtails down her back. Today she is conceded to be one of the greatest players of all time. California gave us another young star in 1924, Helen Jacobs, a husky little miss of 16 who marched to victory in the National Girls' Championship. She is of the magnetic, fiery type, reminiscent of McLoughlin, rather than the calm, placid maiden-like Miss Wills. Helen Jacobs has gameness, personality and physique. She should go far on the road to the Championship.

The East, particularly New York, Philadelphia and Boston, has produced few girls with real promise until the last five years. Suddenly interest sprung up, and since 1920 new and promising players are appearing with encouraging frequency. This revival of interest is due to three things.

1. *The success of and willingness to play of Molla Mallory.*

2. *The return to competition and wonderful personal interest of Mrs. Hazel Wightman.*

3. *The organization and development of women's tournaments by Mrs. Wightman and Miss Florence Ballin.*

One cannot overestimate the service rendered by the personal instruction Mrs. Wightman gave to scores of girls in the East. She is the source of the success of Mrs. Marion Zinderstein Jessup and in my opinion largely responsible for Helen Wills' gaining the championship as soon as she did. Miss Helen Wills would have gained the crown sooner or later, but Mrs. Wightman, in 1923, stepped in and in a few weeks rubbed off the edges, bolstered the weaknesses and polished up Miss Wills' game to a point where she won the coveted title, which she has since held. Mrs. Wightman, while herself the greatest of all women net players, stresses the value of the drive and ground game, without which no net attack can succeed.

Women's Tennis

I am sure that in the face of the evidence one cannot dispute the statement that the ideal game for a woman tennis player is the baseline driving game, with the ability to volley where the opportunity offers for a certain kill. If ever women can cover court as fast as men, or hit as hard, then let them use the all-court game and let men watch out, for remember that Kipling has confided to us that the female of the species is deadlier than the male.

CHAPTER X

THE GAME AND THE COURT

EVERYTIME I find myself playing tennis under new conditions I wish I knew more about the game itself. We group many games under the term "tennis." They are all played under the same rules and in the same spirit but they are not the same game. There is grass court tennis, clay, sand and dirt court tennis (euphoniously grouped under "clay"), hard court (asphalt, concrete and cement) and indoor (linoleum-wood) tennis. Each and every one of these surfaces require a different technique and different shots, yet all are grouped under the name "tennis," and the greatest of these is "grass."

Some players vary in skill according to the surface of the court. Manuel Alonso, always one of the great players of the world,

TWO OF WILLIAM M. JOHNSTON'S SHOTS

At left, end of a backhand, made with perfect footwork and balance. At right, "Little Bill" smacks a shoulder-high forehand drive; his eyes are on the ball and his footwork permits the shifting of weight at the moment of impact.

PLATE 45

TWO SNAPS OF THE 1924 WIMBLEDON WINNER

Jean Borotra of France illustrates the play that enabled him to beat Vincent Richards in their match on the Centre Court.

PLATE 46

is one of the first three or four on clay.
Ichiya Kumagae was almost a class better
on clay than on grass. Bill Johnston is the
premier player of the world on hard courts.
Frank T. Anderson is among the top flight
men in the United States on wood. Wallace
Johnson, wonderful on grass, is a class worse
on dirt and almost mediocre on wood or
hard courts. Personally, I spend most of
my time when playing on wood or hard
courts in wondering what the game is all
about. Yet during the past ten years, during
which period I have played on all sorts and
conditions of courts, in all sorts and conditions of places, certain facts have been borne
in on me quite forcibly. My ideas are at
variance with most people's concerning the
so-called "speed" of the game on different
surfaces. Most people judge "speed" by
the speed of the ball as it bounds off the
ground. I judge the speed of the game by
the amount of time a player has to make his
return before the ball bounds the second

time. Following this standard I place the court surfaces as follows:

1. Wood, the fastest game of all;
2. Linoleum;
3. Grass;
4. Hard Courts;
5. Dirt.

My reason for this classification is that wood provides the lowest and shortest bounce and dirt the highest and longest, the others varying in that order. Thus it will be seen that grass is the fastest of outdoor tennis. Contrary to general belief, the average bound on a dirt court is far higher than that on asphalt or cement. The speed of shot required outdoors varies conversely with the service; the harder the surface, the slower and longer the bounds, the faster the shot required to win. Thus speed of shot is not so essential on grass as it is on dirt or hard courts. This is not true where speed is the big factor. Indoor tennis is always handicapped by rather inferior lighting, even under the best of conditions. Speed will win in bad light always. On both wood and linoleum spin is almost useless, therefore speed will prove the deciding factor in the majority of cases.

Grass tennis is the height of skill, for on grass spin, change of pace, speed control, placement and steadiness, all play their true part and carry their correct value. Grass tennis may be won by strength, finesse, subtlety or a combination of all. There is no stroke in the game that is seriously handicapped on grass. Therefore grass tennis has been and still is the standard of championship play. I regret to say that I fear it is doomed in the near future, owing to the tremendous expense of upkeep and the comparatively small area where grass courts are practical.

Clay or dirt courts are the most universal of all surfaces. This game is capable of almost as great variation of tactics as grass, but certain forms of offense are handicapped or almost nullified by the surface. Speed

155

still carries its own reward, but twist and subtle short placements are seriously injured because the bounce is so high that a player has time to reach the ball. The chop stroke, most valuable on grass, is under a distinct disadvantage on clay or dirt because, instead of shooting off the ground, it stops, hesitates and rises in its bound. Drop shots and stop-volleys are almost useless. Sound driving is the best clay court game. The arguments against the clay court game are more true in the United States than in Europe where they understand the care of dirt courts better than we. In the United States the idea of a perfect clay court is one baked solid, so hard that there is no resiliency to the surface. Nothing could be worse from a tennis player's angle. The ideal clay court should provide a bound approximating a grass court. The ball on the average drive should bound waist high. Most clay courts in America bring the ball to you shoulder-high or above. The ideal clay court should be slightly spongy, dark in color, and damp, so there is no dust. The main difficulty in the United States is to convince the groundsmen at the clubs that clay or dirt courts need water. If the clay court is kept moist, then the game comes as close to grass court tennis as it is possible to provide without grass.

Hard court tennis is a game of speed, speed and then speed. I have tried the defensive, waiting game on the courts of California, always to my sorrow. Finesse is useless, spin, other than topspin to hold the light balls, is useless. Chop strokes, soft placements and drop shots have no place in the hard court player's game. It is drive, smash and volley. Punch everything as soon as possible. Hard courts are the obvious answer to the games of Maurice McLoughlin, R. L. Murray, Elia Fottrell, John R. Strachan, and to the forehand of Bill Johnston. One wonders how such players as Howard Kinsey and Bob Kinsey developed on these courts. Hard courts are a wonderful aid to offense and attack, but the well-rounded, all court game is almost impossible to use.

The indoor game, whether on wood or linoleum, is a game of speed. Twist is nullified by the surface. Even topspin is more or less useless. Flat fast ground-strokes, stiff hard volleys and a speedy service—these are the shots to use. The one stroke that gains vast importance over the outdoor game is the half volley, which can be played with certainty owing to the perfect surface and lack of wind variation indoors. One reason for the outstanding ability of Vincent Richards in the indoor game is his ability to half volley.

Hard courts and dirt courts tend to lighten the balls by wearing off the nap of the cover. For this reason excessive topspin is used to control the light ball in its flight. The grass court tends to make a ball heavier and has little effect on the type of stroke used. The indoor game has little or no effect on the ball, but the surface itself forces spin out of use and develops the flat shot.

The time is coming when tennis must be standardized. The grass court game is passing. I must admit this truth, greatly as I deplore it. It will not be long, possibly twenty-five years, before grass courts will be a rarity, and all Championships will be played on clay or some dirt surface. The time has come for the International Federation, of which the United States is now a member, to take up the question of what particular surface, clay or dirt court, will be recognized as the standard. It should be dark in color, capable of retaining moisture, and of a consistency that will be soft, springy but not slippery. This court surface once chosen could then be included in the equipment of all clubs looking for championship events in the future. The En-Tout-Cas court seems almost ideal. The surface of certain clay courts in the United States, notably those at the Hartford Golf Club, the Triple A at St. Louis, the Orange Lawn Tennis Club, the Montclair A. C. and the University Club of Cleveland are worthy of consideration. St. Cloud, outside of Paris, has the most beautiful dirt courts I have ever seen. It is not so important which of several types of surface is chosen, however, as it is that the selection be made, so that clubs may start to put in a standardized court.

The indoor court is rapidly coming to the fore. The time is not far distant when every city of importance will have a fine indoor club. The demand will force the supply. I am convinced that battleship linoleum is the ideal indoor surface. It is dark in color, true in bound and, while fast, does not have the extreme shoot that spoils the wood game. I am a great believer in speed but there is a limit to the speed a human being may attain. Wood is too fast for a man to attain command of strokes and hold it long, if compelled to handle the bound off wood.

The most important item, other than surface, in indoor tennis is light. Most indoor courts are under-lit. It is far better to have too much light than too little.

Unless standardization of courts comes very soon, I think that ranking by court surface should be made. It is working an injustice to many players to over-stress the grass court game, when over 90 per cent of tennis is played on dirt, clay or hard courts. I look to see the day when we have a classification of players by grass, clay, hard and indoor court play.

CHAPTER XI

VARIETY IS THE SPICE OF LIFE

This article was written late in 1918 and published in AMERICAN LAWN TENNIS *of March 15, 1919. It is included in this book to show how the author's views at that time pointed the way to his success today.—Editor.*

"VARIETY is the spice of life" a famous author once remarked. He was probably correct about life, and is certainly correct about that small portion of existence known as tennis. Variety, or versatility, is the spice, essence and cardinal principle of tennis success.

The great players of the recent decade have been examples of versatility. They always "united their game." No better example of this can be found than R. N. Williams, 2nd, the greatest player of the age, in the opinion of the writer. Williams was essentially a baseline player. He preferred to play his shots off the rising bounce of his opponent's ground strokes. Yet, once let

162

Williams see that his baseline game was not working, and he immediately began a net attack, where he varied his old style completely. I do not mean Williams ever stooped to modify his strokes, for he would not. He merely changed the style of his game while still adhering to form, which he placed above all else.

This is what should be remembered by all young players. It is quite possible to change the style of your game without letting down or playing incorrect shots. The great mistake made by many novices is to forsake form the moment they start to lose.

Many people will tell you that it is possible to have too many strokes. Believe me, that is a fallacy; no one can know or play too many strokes, provided that person knows how each shot is made and when to use it. The "why" and the "wherefor" of every shot must become second nature to them before a shot can be truthfully considered part of their game.

There are, in tennis, at the present time sev-

eral prominent players who would be improved at least fifty per cent. if they took
the trouble to learn the "why and wherefor"
of their game. The reason Frederick B.
Alexander is the wonderful player that he
is, is mainly because he never makes a stroke
without a definite idea of what he is trying
to do with it. The object to be attained determines the shot Alexander plays. In nine
cases out of ten, even among the ranking
players, the shot played is the essential, and
the object attained by it determined not by
design but chance.

The forehand and backhand drive, so often
miscalled "Lawford," the forehand and
backhand chop, the volley, deep or short,
the overhead smash and service constitute all
tennis strokes. Every other shot is but an
outgrowth or variation of these. The "trap"
shot or half volley, commonly known as
"pickup," is but a slightly delayed volley,
and governed by the same method of play.

The order for a beginner to take up these
strokes of course varies with the viewpoint

of the instructor, but to my mind the soundest method is:

(1) Drive.
(2) Service.
(3) Volley and smash.
(4) Chop.

Why? Well, the drive, fore- or backhand, is the foundation of every tennis game. Therefore, lay your foundation first. Lay it sound and sure.

The drive is hit with a full arm swing and practically stiff wrist; therefore, when learning, do not mix it with the chop, that is hit with a short, cramped swing and decided wrist motion.

Service is essential, therefore learn it as soon as possible.

The net game is the structure that you raise on the foundation of your drive. This is the winning punch, but it is useless unless your foundation is good enough to allow you to meet a moderate attack and take the offensive yourself; therefore you cannot learn to go to the net until after the ground game is developed to a moderate degree.

The chop stroke is either an ornament to your attack or else a secondary defense and can afford to wait until your game is solidly built.

The only way to develop the game in this order is to first grasp the four fundamentals that apply to all strokes:

(1) Keep your eye on the ball;

(2) The body must be at right angles to the net and the shoulders parallel to the line of flight of the ball;

(3) The weight must always travel into the stroke, that is, from back to front foot;

(4) The shot must never be hurried or cramped.

These essentials once learned, take each shot by itself and work on that only. The drive cannot be learned while you are also studying the volley. Stay on the baseline and drive everything, whether or not you miss them. When learning the volley and smash, go to the net at every opportunity and carefully study the relation of your return

166

to the angle of your opponent's return and cover the most natural angle for his stroke. When you reach the chop, chop everything. Time enough to "mix 'em up" after you have mastered the stroke.

Thus, practice should be a careful plugging away at a single shot until that shot is learned thoroughly.

Tournament or match play is exactly the opposite. In practice you always do the same thing. In match play never do the expected, unless it is simply a case of "putting the ball in play."

The two greatest things in match play are to put the ball in play and never give the other man the shot he likes to play. Remember that 80 per cent. of all the points in tennis as a whole are lost by errors, not won by earned points. Therefore, by always making your opponent play shots he does not like to play, you will swell his error column, and his errors count for you just as much as your earned points. If he can't handle a chop, then chop to him. If he hurries his stroke against a net man, go up at every opportunity.

Only do not do any one thing so much that he gets used to it, for its effectiveness is gone just as soon as he solves the problem. One must always mix one's game against Ichiya Kumagae, the famous Japanese star, because he can find a speedy antidote for any stroke that bothers him.

The ability to vary one's game is not in the racquet work alone. It is largely mental. One must change one's mental attitude with every change of stroke. When you drive, think "drive"; when you chop, put all your mind on chop. Do not chop with a drive still in your brain. You will miss your shot. The ability to change a mental attitude with each shot requires absolute concentration.

There is more to this question than merely mixing strokes. There is the far greater one of changing the style of one's game. In general, never change your style when ahead. Do not take chances when winning! The time to take chances is when you are losing! Do not change your game if you lose a set,

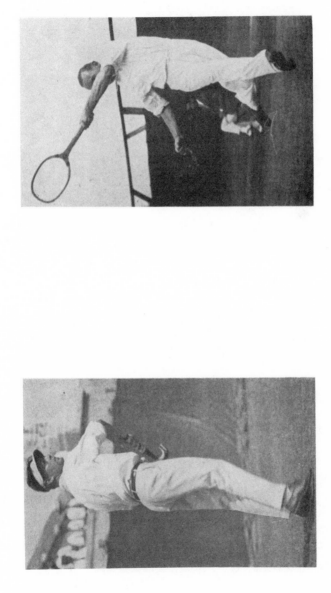

AN AMERICAN AND AN ANTIPODEAN

Howard Kinsey (at left) completes his "loop drive" at Forest Hills; note the strange body and arm position. John B. Hawkes, at the Orange L. T. C., finishes a drive while clear off the ground.

PLATE 47

RIVALS IN MANY MATCHES

Wallace F. Johnson (at left) gives a perfect example of his peculiar under-cut forehand. Watson Washburn (at right) takes a low volley from close to the net.

PLATE 48

provided that set is close, 6-3 for example, where a service is lost once. If that set were 6-1 or 6-0, and you have been playing anywhere near form, then change your game at once, for you are outclassed with the original type and might just as well take a chance.

The whole secret of tennis success outside of actual stroke perfection (which any one can learn in time) is to always keep mentally alert. "Use the bean" at all times and under all conditions. When you guess wrong, you will look a fool and get called "bonehead"; but never mind, for you gain more than you lose, even if no recognition is taken of it.

The main key to the phenomenal success and progress of Vincent Richards, the 1917 and 1918 Boys' National Champion and holder of the 1918 Junior National Doubles and Men's National Doubles, is his brilliant brain that is working every moment the boy is on the court.

Verily, in tennis, variety, both of strokes and mental attitude, is the spice and essential of tennis life.

CHAPTER XII

PACE AND SPEED

In the May 15, 1919, *issue of* AMERICAN LAWN TENNIS *an article entitled "Pace and Speed" by W. T. Tilden, 2nd, appeared and, like the author's "Variety" article, it was widely discussed. It is now republished exactly as it appeared.—Editor.*

MANY tennis followers and players speak knowingly of the "speed" and "pace" on the shots of certain famous exponents of the game. Nine out of every ten persons use the two words as synonyms. They interchange them indiscriminately and lightly speak of the "pace" of T. R. Pell's backhand and the "speed" of W. A. Larned's drive.

"Speed" and "Pace" are very different things. They are related, but are in no way the same thing.

"Speed" is measured by the time required by the flight of the ball through the air.

"Pace" is the momentum (speed plus player's weight) with which the ball comes off the ground from its bounce. It is timing. It is solidity of stroke. "Speed" is an ornament on the structure of one's game. "Pace" is the foundation on which the game is built.

The bounce of differently speeded strokes will vary little, but a change of paces causes a totally different sensation on the racquet at the impact of the ball. A player may hit a very fast drive by a wild swing of his arm, yet it will carry no pace, as his weight placement is out of the shot and not in it. An example of a very fast, yet little "paced" drive is the terrific wallop that Harold A. Throckmorton delights in when he receives the ball shoulder high on his forehand. This shot goes like a streak of light, yet on reaching the ground bounds high and comparatively slowly, because there is no body weight behind the stroke. In marked contrast to this is the forehand "poke" drive of F. B. Alexander, which travels more slowly through the air, but gains momentum off the bound, owing to Alexander having thrown his body weight behind his swing.

The most notable example of excessive pace within the knowledge of modern tennis players was William A. Larned. Every one who played Larned found themselves hitting his drives late, and thus continually slicing out the sideline. It was not the fault of the player; the answer lay in the peculiarly fast "heavy" bound of Larned's drive that came so rapidly that his opponent misjudged it by making his guess by the air flight. There is true "pace" in that drive of Larned. Some players have it today, although none to the marked degree of Larned. Chief among the men who achieve real pace are William M. Johnston, to a less degree R. N. Williams, 2nd, Charles S. Garland, F. B. Alexander and others. Pace is really nothing more than the best way of acquiring the maximum result with the minimum effort.

Some men have both great speed and pace. One tends to produce the other, yet they can be separate. R. L. Murray has speed at all times off his forehand, but only acquires "pace" at certain times.

Pace and Speed

Pace is a far more useful adjunct to a tennis game than speed, but judicial combination of the two is necessary for any first flight man. It is not what the ball does in the air half as much as what it does off the ground that counts. Speed is only vital against a man at the net and "pace" will at least force a man to volley correctly to hold the ball in court, while speed needs only a "block" to stop it and put it back.

So with apologies to Omar:

The secret of success lies in good pace;
Speed may look well and help you save your
face.
Yet if one really wants to reach the top,
Remember this, 'Tis pace that holds the Ace.

CHAPTER XIII

GREATNESS IN MATCH PLAY

*Early in 1924, for his "Passing Shots"
department in* AMERICAN LAWN TENNIS, *the
author wrote the following article. It con-
tains so much of real value that it is repro-
duced.—Editor.*

WHAT is a great tennis player? By
that I mean a great match player.
The question came in the course of a fan
fest I had at Buffalo with Cedric Major, and
his reply was most interesting. He said:

"A great tennis player is one with ability
to 'scramble'."

For a moment I thought he was discussing
eggs, and then I realized that he had placed
his finger on one of the real essentials of the
great match player. What he meant was the
ability of a player to go out after the impossible shot and return it in the pinch, return
it, no matter how, but still return.

I am a great believer in style and form,
but when the ultimate show-down comes,

174

when the crisis is at hand, it is results and not style that wins. "Scrambling" well expresses the real vital point. Watch Billy Johnston, Vincent Richards, Wallace Johnson or Manuel Alonso, our leading "scramblers," and see them discard form stroke and any other piece of tennis technique to return an seemingly impossible shot. They sprawl over the court, even at times using two hands if caught, but they put back that ball. I well remember a marvelous two-handed pickup shot of Billy Johnston's in 1920 when I led him 2 sets to 1 and 5-3 in the final of the National Championship. I smashed at his feet, a certain winner, yet Johnston "scrambled" his way to the ball and pushed it back with two hands. It saved him the set, which he ultimately won. His ultimate defeat had no bearing on the case, for if he had not made that shot he was lost, 3 sets to 1.

Many times Richards has pulled out matches that seemed hopelessly lost by scrambling a shot with no idea except the one of putting back the ball. It is impossible to overstress the value of playing every point until it is hopelessly lost. Many fine players, notably N. W. Niles, Craig Biddle and R. N. Williams, 2nd, have lost vital matches because they will not scramble at the expense of form. Tennis is a game of result. Put back the ball in a match, even if you do it with no more effective weapon than the handle or frame of your racquet. Cedric Major showed wisdom and analysis when he summed up the great match player as the one who has the ability to scramble in the pinch.

What is a great service? The general idea of a great service is one of blinding speed and terrific spin. Usually such a delivery comes up to the definition of a great service, yet I would give another thought to add to it.

In my opinion a great service is one which is difficult to return. It is not a matter of speed or twist alone. It is a question of brains. No one will attempt to deny that the deliveries of Gerald Patterson, R. N.

Williams, Howard Voshell and Willis Davis are great, yet what about those of Zenzo Shimizu, Wallace Johnson, John B. Hawkes and in the old days Harold Hackett? This latter group seem to push the ball over the net with little or no real speed or even twist, yet so cleverly are they placed, so subtly are they twisted, that it is seldom that the receiver can do more than defend it, and often he actually misses his return. I consider these men in the latter group possessors of great deliveries. Billy Johnston partially represents both groups, yet he is hardly to be placed in either; but certainly his service is great.

The first type may thrill a gallery far more than the second, yet I do not regard them as essentially greater. The only requisite of a great service is that it wins. Whether the result is derived from speed, twist or placement is a matter of no account. The truly great server is the man who combines all three assets and then mixes them up with a sound judgment according to the man he is playing.